MEZZE SMALL PLATES TO SHARE

MEZZE SMALL PLATES TO SHARE

dips ◆ salads ◆ pastries ◆ sweets

RYLAND PETERS & SMALL

LONDON ◆ NEW YORK

Senior Designer Toni Kay
Commissioning Editor Nathan Joyce
Production Controller David Hearn
Art Director Leslie Harrington
Editorial Director Julia Charles
Publisher Cindy Richards

Prop Stylist Joanna Harris
Food Stylist Seiko Hatfield
Assistant Food Stylist Lola Milne
Indexer Vanessa Bird

First published in 2015 by
Ryland Peters & Small
20–21 Jockey's Fields
London WC1R 4BW
and
341 E 116th St
New York NY 10029

www.rylandpeters.com

Text © Ghillie Başan 2015
Design and photographs
© Ryland Peters & Small 2015

ISBN: 978-1-84975-651-8

10 9 8 7 6 5 4 3 2 1

A CIP record for this book is available
from the British Library.

US Library of Congress CIP data has been
applied for.

Printed and bound in China

Notes

• When a recipe calls for the grated zest of
citrus fruit, buy unwaxed fruit and wash
well before using. If you can only find
treated fruit, scrub well in warm soapy
water before using.

• Ovens should be preheated to the
specified temperatures. We recommend
using an oven thermometer. If using
a fan-assisted oven, adjust temperatures
according to the manufacturer's
instructions.

• To sterilize a preserving jar, wash it in hot,
soapy water and rinse in boiling water.
Place in a large saucepan and cover with
hot water. With the saucepan lid on,
bring the water to a boil and continue
boiling for 15 minutes. Turn off the heat
and leave the jar in the water until just
before filling. Invert the jars onto a clean
tea/dish towel to dry. Sterilize the lids
for 5 minutes, by boiling or according
to the manufacturer's instructions. Jars
should be filled and sealed while they
are still hot.

CONTENTS

INTRODUCTION

If I told you that in the month of July, the height of the tourist season, I sat alone on a long stretch of beach looking across the still, turquoise water of the Blue Lagoon in southwest Turkey without a soul in sight, you wouldn't believe me. Sheltered from the open sea, the Lagoon was once a secret gem but now, fringed with hotels and bars, it is a busy nature park, with rentable sun-chairs, crowds of bathers and mooring yachts, and the water is no longer crystal clear. The time I sat there, though, drinking in the silence mixed with the warm, sunbaked aromas and bright colours of the coastline – saffron and ivory butterflies, wild scarlet poppies dotted amongst the pungent mountain thyme, and the reddish-purple of the glass of cherry juice in my hand – it was 1984 and I was having mezze with my feet dipped in the Mediterranean Sea.

I had come by bus from Pamukkale where the hot springs and polished white calcium-formed travertines perch like a marble castle gleaming in the sunlight above the cotton fields and fertile Anatolian plains. The only visible signs of life along the way had been the brightly head-scarfed women working in the fields, a few passing trucks and donkey-driven carts, and the haphazard construction of restaurants and hotels on the track winding down the pine-forested hillside to the Lagoon. At one point on the hot, sticky bus journey, the driver had veered alarmingly close to a pick-up truck bulging with freshly picked tomatoes, close enough for the skinny ticket-collector to lean, precariously, out of the door and skim the ruby fruit off the top. Holding onto the doorframe with one hand, he chucked the tomatoes into the bus with the other to a spirited reception of claps and blessings to Allah, while delighted passengers scooped them up and bit into the sweet juice. As the stuffy air in the bus had become somewhat stifling, I was convinced that these tomatoes were the juiciest any God had ever created.

A little while later, relaxing in the tranquillity of the Lagoon, a selection of mezze was laid out before me – little bowls of feta drizzled with olive oil and sprinkled with oregano; puréed smoked aubergine/eggplant combined with yogurt, lemon and garlic in a velvety dip; artichoke bottoms stuffed with succulent cinnamon rice and wrapped in tender vine leaves; freshly fried salt-and-pepper squid with a creamy pine-nut sauce; a fresh crunchy salad of skinned tomatoes, cucumber, onions and handfuls of chopped parsley tossed in sour pomegranate syrup; and a round of freshly baked flatbread sprinkled with nigella seeds. This was food to share, savour and swoon over. It was too good to eat alone. With every mouthful and every sigh of sublime pleasure, I thought about eating my way into the remote pockets of Turkey and the Middle East to immerse myself in the culinary culture of the region. I thought about travelling and writing, cooking and sharing, and I thought about capturing that very moment – the moment that a mouthful of mezze changed the course of my life.

Several decades later and with many miles of mezze under my belt, I still go back in my mind to that memorable day at the Lagoon, partly because I remember every deliciously tantalizing bite; the food was so fresh and simple, so lacking in pretence, and so fitting to its relaxed environment. The only thing wrong with that day was that I was eating the mezze alone. By its very nature, mezze needs to be shared. It is a custom that lends itself to good company and unabashed indulgence.

My first experience of eating genuine home-cooked mezze was in the ancient city of Bursa, the first seat of the Ottoman Empire. It was in the home of one of my English students, a middle-aged opera singer, which was a novelty in itself. Her modest home was located up a steep narrow street lined with rickety, wooden houses, some raised up on stilts, others set firmly in the mud. Her door was painted turquoise blue to ward off the evil eye and there were ornate, rusting bars over the open windows through which the strains of Italian opera trickled like clear honey on stale bread – an alien sound amongst the noise of children laughing and screaming, cars and mopeds honking and tooting, and the tinny sound of Turkish music emanating from scratched cassette tapes.

My hosts (the opera singer and her 3 daughters) greeted me with excited anticipation, thrusting a pair of dainty bright orange fluffy slippers at my feet so that I could remove my dirty shoes before entering their immaculate home, with its polished floor tiles and erect chairs positioned in the traditional manner around the perimeter of the salon. Here, sitting in the chair of honour with my feet looking like large fish stuffed into the two halves of a stout loaf, I was given a tulip-shaped glass of tea while my hostess and her well-fed daughters squeezed into the tiny kitchen, not much bigger than a good-sized broom cupboard, to finish off the preparations of the local mezze. There were beef tartare balls, prepared with 30 different spices and served on lettuce leaves with a squeeze of lemon; pickled stuffed aubergines/eggplants; cigar-shaped cheese pastries flavoured with dill; roasted baby (bell) peppers stuffed with cheese and oregano; bean salad with a tahini

dressing; tiny lamb kebabs/kabobs wrapped in a flat bread parcel; and sweet saffron pears. Naturally I tried everything, delighting my own palate with fire and flavour, soothed by the syrup of the poached pears, but what I had yet to understand was that this was not a meal; this was simply hospitality. It was mezze in its purest form – small, tasty portions shared and enjoyed at leisure in the late afternoon for the sole purpose of welcoming and pleasing a guest.

One of the wonderful things to learn about mezze is that there are no rules. It can be enjoyed by anyone at any time of the day, presented as a snack, an appetizer to a meal, or as a buffet spread, with the unspoken understanding that the food is served in small quantities to be shared at a leisurely pace so that you feel invigorated, inspired and sublimely contented. There are cold mezze dishes, hot ones, and there are even sweet ones, often served in sequence but, on occasion, they are laid out on the table together. The Arabic word 'mezze' or 'mazza' ('meze' in Turkish) is derived from the ancient Persian word 'maza', meaning 'taste' or 'relish', which is exactly what mezze is – something tasty to be savoured at leisure with the aim of delighting the palate, not to fill the belly.

Enjoyed by the ancient Greeks, Romans, Persians, the medieval Arabs and the Ottoman Turks, mezze is at the heart and sole of culinary life in Turkey, the Middle East and parts of North Africa. A feast for the eyes as well as for the palate, mezze is steeped in a fascinating history of ancient empires and dynasties, wars and diverse religions, and the east-west trade routes, all of which have had a lasting influence on the culinary cultures of this vast and turbulent region. Traditionally designed to tickle the palate and soak up the intoxicating wine and spirits, mezze was indulged in by the early travellers, traders and the noble elite, who were entertained with music, singing and dancing and, often, the ensuing sexual activities. Mezze was an institution, a way of life, a method of socializing, and the drinking of alcohol was at the root of its philosophy. The conversion to Islam from the seventh century onwards altered this philosophy by prohibiting the consumption of alcohol and curbing the association between food and sex amongst devout Muslims, but the tradition of mezze and musical merriment continued.

In daily life, the role of mezze is buoyant, like a moveable feast. It presents itself in song and in poetry, at religious festivals and family celebrations, as an offering of hospitality, and as a snack in the busy streets and markets. Throughout the day, you can embark on a mezze voyage, eating your way around a city and the ideal places to scoop up some inspiration are the busy bazaars and souks of Istanbul, Aleppo, Beirut, Cairo and Marrakesh. Arguably, the best mezze is to be found in Lebanon and Turkey as the cuisines of both countries are held in high esteem – a legacy of the Arab and Ottoman empires. There have been many other culinary influences throughout the history of the whole Middle Eastern region, stretching into North Africa in one direction, into Greece and the Balkan countries in another, and beyond Iran and the Caspian Sea so, from a historic and cultural point of view, the whole region is fascinating; from a culinary perspective it is in a class of its own and mezze nestles proudly at its very core.

Some of the best mezze I have ever had has been in hidden cafés tucked behind rural market stalls, the food literally arriving from the fields and orchards to the plate. The mezze produced in the humblest of homes in arid terrain or war-torn towns has often been the most surprising and uplifting, but the most unusual mezze invitation I have ever received during all my years of living and travelling in the region was to a picnic in a hamam, the traditional Turkish bath house. Bathing on the steaming hot slabs of marble, women of all ages started to sing and dance with their breasts and buttocks wobbling and swinging, while they unpacked baskets filled with olives, pickles, a gypsy salad of peppers, onions and white cheese, and an assortment of savoury pastries, still warm from the communal oven. This extraordinary feast of 'hamam meze', simple food enjoyed with a merry group of naked women unabashedly washing and talking animatedly through

the steam, has been for ever imprinted on my mind, and picnics have never been quite the same since!

Aromatic, fragrant, spicy and moreish, mezze may be an ancient custom, but it has a modern twist. It is the epitome of modern eating – small portions, healthy ingredients, food to share – to be enjoyed at the family kitchen table, on the veranda, in an elaborate dining room, outside in the shade of an old fig tree, or even in the hamam! In this book, I have brought together a selection of the traditional and the modern, some classics and some of my own creations, in the hope you will enjoy creating your own balance of tastes and flavours with the savoury bursts culminating in a crescendo of sweetness. Of all the cookery workshops I run in my home and abroad, the mezze ones are the most popular, as it is the kind of food that involves everyone; there is something for every taste bud, and the joy is infectious. Mezze is not simply an appetizer – it is much more than that – so it is important to embrace the original philosophy that it brings people together to socialize, to eat and drink, and to share. With the recipes in this book, I hope you can escape in your imagination and take a culinary journey in the company of good friends because, wherever you are in the world, the tradition of mezze is a gift and, if you enjoy sharing tasty dishes with others, then it is a tradition worth exploring.

BASIC RECIPES

When it comes to cooking dishes from a culture that is not your own, it is a good idea to become familiar with some of the basic store-cupboard ingredients and methods, as they can make all the difference to the taste of the end product. Here I have included all the basics of my kitchen. I prepare them for my family and for my cookery workshops which means I can rustle up authentic mezze quickly and with the greatest of ease.

Harissa

Harissa and other fiery pastes made with dried red chillies/chiles and spices are used to flavour mezze throughout the Mediterranean region. Of North African origin, harissa is a versatile paste and can be used as a condiment as well as a flavouring, often combined with finely chopped fresh coriander/cilantro or flat-leaf parsley, dried mint or oregano, or the finely chopped peel of preserved lemon or bitter orange. I keep a batch in the refrigerator to whip out as a condiment or to combine with other ingredients to make instant mezze. Remember that a little goes a long way!

approximately 12 long dried red
   chillies/chiles (Horn or New
   Mexico are ideal varieties)
2 teaspoons cumin seeds
2 teaspoons coriander seeds
3–4 garlic cloves, chopped
1–2 teaspoons sea salt
2–3 tablespoons olive oil

Makes 2–3 tablespoons

Place the chillies/chiles in a bowl and pour over enough boiling water to cover them. Leave them to soak for about 48 hours, changing the water from time to time. Dry roast the cumin and coriander seeds and grind them to a powder using a pestle and mortar.

Drain the chillies/chiles, chop off the stalks, and squeeze out most of the seeds. Discard the stalks and seeds (but leave a few of the latter, depending on the desired heat), and coarsely chop the chillies/chiles. Using a pestle and mortar, pound the chillies/chiles with the garlic and salt to form a thick, smooth paste – this takes some time, but it is well worth the effort.

Beat in the ground spices and pound the paste again. Beat in half the oil and, at this stage, if desired, you can add other ingredients, such as finely chopped fresh coriander/cilantro, mint or oregano, or finely chopped dried orange peel.

Spoon the mixture into a sterilized jar and pour over the rest of the oil. Seal the jar and store it in a cool place, or in the refrigerator. It will keep for 1–2 months – just use a little as and when you need it.

Zahtar

Zahtar is the Arabic word for thyme, which grows wild in the hills of the eastern Mediterranean region. It is also the word for the tasty spice mix made with dried thyme, ground sumac berries, roasted sesame seeds and salt, and it is sprinkled over bread, cheese, yogurt and salads. It is a favourite seasoning for street vendors and it is a handy mix to have in the kitchen to sprinkle over cubes of feta, freshly cooked halloumi, grilled meatballs and roasted vegetables.

4 tablespoons dried wild thyme
2 tablespoons ground sumac
2 tablespoons roasted sesame seeds
1 tablespoon sea salt

Makes 8 tablespoons

Mix the ingredients together in a bowl, rubbing them with your fingers to release the aromas. Tip the mixture into a sterilized jar and seal tightly. Store in a cool place for up to 6 weeks.

Dukkah

Derived from the Arabic word for 'to pound', dukkah ('duqqa') is prepared by pounding the ingredients using a pestle and mortar rather than grinding, so that there is texture as well as flavour in the spice mix. The ingredients vary according to the region, but the base mix will include sesame seeds, coriander and cumin seeds, roasted hazelnuts or pistachios and salt; sometimes dried mint, dried chilli or roasted chickpeas are added. For a quick traditional snack, you simply bind two tablespoons of dukkah with the same quantity of olive oil and dip chunks of warm, crusty bread into it. I always have a batch of homemade dukkah in the kitchen cupboard to sprinkle over crunchy salads, sautéed vegetables, grilled meat and poultry, and for adding to pulse-/legume-based dishes.

4 tablespoons hazelnuts
2 tablespoons sesame seeds
1 tablespoon coriander seeds
1 tablespoon cumin seeds
1 tablespoon fennel seeds
2 teaspoons fine chilli/hot red
    pepper flakes
2 teaspoons dried mint
1–2 teaspoons sea salt

Makes 6 tablespoons

Dry roast the hazelnuts in a heavy based frying pan/skillet until they emit a nutty aroma. Rub off any loose skins and, using a pestle and mortar, crush them lightly to break them up.

Dry roast the sesame seeds, coriander, cumin, fennel and chilli/hot red pepper flakes together, until they emit a nutty aroma, and add them to the hazelnuts. Crush them all together lightly so that they are well blended but uneven in texture – some almost ground to a powder, others in crunchy bits.

Stir in the mint and sea salt to taste and spoon the mixture into a sterilized, airtight jar and store away from direct sunlight. It will keep for 4–6 weeks.

Zhug

Fiery and versatile like harissa, zhug ('zhoug') is a popular chilli/chile paste in Yemen, Oman, the United Arab Emirates, Saudi Arabia and Egypt. Containing the characteristic flavours of Yemeni cooking – chilli/chile, cardamom and garlic – zhug is usually served as a condiment with grilled and fried vegetables or shellfish, or it is combined with ingredients like pounded tomatoes, the pulped flesh of smoked aubergines/eggplants, or finely chopped grilled (bell) peppers, olive oil and fistfuls of finely chopped coriander/cilantro and served as mezze with chunks of fresh bread to dip into it.

8 dried red chillies/chiles
   (Horn or New Mexico varieties)
4 garlic cloves, roughly chopped
1 teaspoon salt
seeds of 4–6 cardamom pods
1 teaspoon caraway seeds
½ teaspoon black peppercorns
a small bunch fresh flat-leaf parsley,
   finely chopped
a small bunch of fresh coriander/
   cilantro, finely chopped
3–4 tablespoons olive oil or
   sunflower oil

large sterilized glass jar

Makes 4-5 tablespoons

Put the chillies/chiles in a bowl, pour boiling water over them and leave them to soak for at least 6 hours. Drain them, cut off the stalks, squeeze out the seeds, and roughly chop them.

Using a pestle and mortar, pound the chillies/chiles with the garlic and salt to a thick, smooth paste. Add the cardamom and caraway seeds and the peppercorns and pound them with the chilli paste – you want to break up the seeds and peppercorns, but they don't have to be perfectly ground as a little bit of texture is good. Beat in the parsley and coriander/cilantro and bind the mixture with the oil.

Spoon the spice paste into a sterilized jar, drizzle the rest of the oil over the top and keep it in a cool place, or in the refrigerator, for up to 4 weeks. When serving as a condiment or a dip for bread, mix the layer of oil into it and garnish with finely chopped coriander/cilantro or parsley.

Samna (clarified butter)

Traditionally, butter was made in a churn fashioned from the tanned skin of a whole goat. Partially filled with milk and tied at the ends, the skin was suspended by four ropes and the woman of the household would jerk it to and fro until the milk was churned. Butter was lavishly used in the cooking of the Medieval and Ottoman periods and clarifying it was the best method of preserving it. Called 'samna' ('samneh') in Arabic, clarified butter (also known as ghee) not only stores for a long time, it also imparts a delicious nutty flavour and aroma to both sweet and savoury dishes.

450 g/4 sticks butter
muslin/cheesecloth

Makes 350 g/12 oz.

To make a batch of samna at home all you need is a block of butter and a small heavy-based saucepan.

Cut the butter into chunks and put them into the saucepan. Melt the butter gently over a very low heat so that it does not brown. Allow the melted butter to froth gently until the fat is as transparent as a teardrop then take it off the heat and leave it to settle before straining it through a piece of muslin/cheesecloth to remove the impurities. Discard any milky solids at the bottom of the saucepan. Store the samna in a clean, sealed container in a cool place, or in the refrigerator, to use in place of butter or oil. You can keep the samna for at least 6 months; many people keep it for longer.

Preserved lemons

Most commonly associated with North Africa, particularly in Moroccan tagines, preserved lemons are used throughout the Middle East. Sometimes they are preserved in brine, vinegar or oil, but the flavour of the salted variety is supreme and, generally, it is only the rind that is used, very finely chopped or finely sliced. The unique, intense lemon flavour enhances many salads, vegetable dishes, and some roasted and grilled dishes, so it is an ideal ingredient to keep in the cupboard for mezze.

8 organic, unwaxed lemons
roughly 8 tablespoons sea salt
freshly squeezed juice of 3–4 lemons
large sterilized glass jar

Wash and dry the lemons and slice the ends off each one. Stand each lemon on one end and make two vertical cuts three-quarters of the way through them, as if cutting them into quarters but keeping the base intact. Stuff a tablespoon of salt into each lemon and pack them into a large sterilized jar. Store the lemons in a cool place for 3–4 days to soften the skins.

Press the lemons down into the jar, so they are even more tightly packed. Pour the freshly squeezed lemon juice over the salted lemons, until they are completely covered. Seal the jar and store it in a cool place for at least a month.

Before using, rinse the salt off the preserved lemons. Cut the lemon into quarters and, using a small sharp knife, remove the salty flesh and discard it. Finely chop or finely slice the rind and use it according to the recipe.

Labna (yogurt cheese)

Yogurt is an ancient and much-valued ingredient throughout the whole of the Middle East and the Mediterranean region. It is easily digestible and nutritious and plays a big role in the daily diet of every community. Thick and creamy, it is often served to accompany other dishes: it is combined with water and a little salt to make the traditional drink 'laban' in Arabic ('ayran' in Turkish) and, particularly in the form of yogurt cheese, it is combined with garlic and other ingredients in many mezze dishes. Yogurt cheese is simply yogurt that has been strained through muslin/cheesecloth for 6–8 hours to thicken it and drain away liquid. It is the consistency of cream cheese or clotted cream. Called 'labna' in the Arabic-speaking countries and 'süzme' in Turkey, it is light and spongy in texture and delectably creamy. Used in both savoury and sweet dishes, it is the foundation of many sumptuous and moreish mezze dips.

1 kg/4 cups thick, creamy yogurt
string or twine
muslin/cheesecloth

Makes 500 g/2 cups

Line a bowl with a large piece of muslin/cheesecloth, overlapping the sides of the bowl, and tip the yogurt into the middle. Pull up the corners of the muslin/cheesecloth and tie them together around a hook, the handle of a wooden spoon, or around the tap/faucet in the kitchen sink, so that you can suspend the muslin/cheesecloth pouch somewhere above the bowl for 6–8 hours. The quantity of yogurt will have reduced by half and you will end up with a little ball of fluffy, white yogurt cheese.

Yogurt cheese balls

You can take the yogurt cheese one step further by leaving it to drain and dry out for 48 hours (in a cool area or in the fridge) then mould it into little balls. Leave the balls to dry out a little more then serve them as a mezze dish drizzled in olive oil combined with a teaspoonful of harissa, or sprinkled with dukkah or zahtar. You can also transfer the plain yogurt cheese balls to a sterilized jar, cover them with plenty of olive oil, and store them in the refrigerator for about 6 days.

Pide with nigella seeds

Throughout the Middle Eastern region, bread is regarded as the food of friendship, a gift from God. Bought daily straight from the baker's oven and torn apart with fingers, it is shared and eaten with practically every meal. Day-old bread is used for cooking and, if it drops to the ground or has to be thrown away, it is first kissed and held to the forehead as a mark of respect. Mezze without bread is almost unthinkable; it is indispensable as a scoop or a mop for all the tasty flavours and juices, enhancing the pleasure of each mouthful. There are many varieties of leavened crusty loaves and flatbreads, but this pide is the first one I had on that memorable day at the Blue Lagoon.

15 g/3 teaspoons fresh yeast, or 7 g/1 x ¼-oz. sachet dried yeast
150 ml/⅔ cup lukewarm water
½ teaspoon granulated sugar
450 g/3 cups unbleached, strong white, or chapati flour
1 teaspoon salt
2 tablespoons olive oil plus a few drops for the bowl
2 tablespoons thick, creamy yogurt
1 egg, beaten
1 tablespoon nigella seeds

Makes 2 medium-sized or 1 large one

Preheat the oven to 220° (425°F) Gas 7.

Put the yeast and the sugar into a small bowl with 2–3 tablespoons of the lukewarm water. Put it aside for about 15 minutes, until it froths.

Sift the flour with the salt into a large bowl. Make a well in the middle and pour in the creamed yeast with the oil, yogurt and the rest of the water. Using your hands, draw in the flour from the sides and work the mixture into a dough, until it leaves the side of the bowl – add more water if necessary, as the dough should be sticky but pliable.

Knead the dough on a lightly floured surface for about 10 minutes, until it is smooth and light. Punch the dough flat, and gather up the edges into the middle, and flip it over. Splash a few drops of oil in the base of large bowl, roll the ball of dough in it, and cover with a damp tea/dish towel. Leave the dough, covered with a damp tea/dish towel, to prove in a warm place for 4–6 hours, or overnight, until it has doubled in size.

Punch the dough down to release the air and knead it again. Lightly oil one large circular, or rectangular, baking sheet, or two smaller ones. Place the dough on a lightly floured surface (divide it into two pieces if you like) and flatten it with the heel of your hand. Use your fingers to stretch it from the middle, creating a thick lip at the edges, until it is as big as your baking sheet. Indent the dough with your fingertips and place it on the baking sheet.

Brush the surface of the dough with a little beaten egg and scatter the nigella seeds over the top. Bake the dough in the preheated oven for about 10 minutes, then reduce the heat to 200°C (400°F) Gas 6 and continue to bake for a further 10 minutes, until the surface is crispy and golden.

Transfer the pide to a wire rack and serve warm, tearing it with your fingers.

COLD MEZZE

With markets selling long, slim aubergines/eggplants the size of a man's forearm, leeks the length of a hockey stick, white pomegranates with resplendent purple seeds, purple carrots with a pale yellow core, ripe figs bursting with sticky juice, unripe green plums to dip in salt, and succulent olives of every hue, mezze is always on the mind in Turkey and the Middle Eastern region. Even the cucumber seller peels you a whole one, quarters it lengthways, and sprinkles it with salt – instant mezze that also acts as a thirst-quencher on a hot day.

Of all the mezze dishes, the cold ones are the simplest. Roasted nuts, marinated olives, cubes of salty cheese, yogurt dips, pickles, salads and fresh fruit are the stalwarts of cold mezze. There are also more time-consuming dishes that involve cooking first and serving cold, such as the traditional 'olive oil' specialties of stuffed vegetables, cured meats and preserved fish.

In a restaurant, mezze dishes are served in sequence of cold, then hot dishes, followed by sweet ones or fresh fruit. In a home, though, you might be served hot and cold together.

NIBBLES

Olives with harissa and preserved lemon

Wherever you find yourself in Greece, Turkey or the Middle East, you will discover that no mezze table is complete without a bowl of olives. Fleshy and juicy, crunchy and bitter, black and wrinkled – everyone has their favourite. Generally bathed in olive oil and flavoured with herbs or spices, olives complement fried hallumi, cubes of feta or a garlicky dip. If you are marinating your own, it is worth looking for either the packets of big, fleshy green olives or the purplish-brown Kalamata olives preserved in brine.

250 g/9 oz. large green, cracked olives or Kalamata olives, soaked in water for 24 hours
2 tablespoons olive oil
1–2 teaspoons Harissa (see page 12)
½ Preserved Lemon (see page 19), finely chopped

Serves 4–6

Drain the olives and, using a sharp knife, cut 3 lengthwise slits in each one if they don't have them already. Pop them into a bowl, mix together the olive oil and harissa, and pour it over the olives. Toss well and scatter the preserved lemon over the top.

If not eating immediately, you can store the olives in a sterilized jar in the refrigerator for 2–3 weeks.

Sweet melon or watermelon with feta

The combination of sweet juicy melon and salty feta is one of those gems you never forget. The key is to choose a sun-ripened melon with honey-sweet flesh, which is not always an easy task if you are shopping in a supermarket. I am often caught sniffing and tapping melons but, once you've tasted the combination in its perfect form, you will understand why!

1 ripe Honeydew or Galia melon, or ½ a ripe watermelon, deseeded and cut into bite-size cubes
200 g/7 oz. feta, rinsed, drained and cut into bite-sized cubes
fresh basil or mint leaves, to garnish

Serves 4–6

Arrange the melon or watermelon on one side of a serving dish with the feta on the other side. Simply serve it with cocktail sticks/toothpicks to pick up a piece of melon and feta together so that you can enjoy the blend of salty sweetness.

If you're serving this dish as a nibble at a party, you can push a cube of melon with a cube of feta onto cocktail sticks/toothpicks so that they are ready just to be picked up and popped into the mouth.

And if you want to combine the melon and feta to make a salad, you can use both types of melon together with the feta, drizzle them in olive oil, and toss them with fresh basil or mint leaves.

Spicy beef tartare and bulgur balls

If you are a fan of 'steak tartare', you will love these little balls from southeastern Turkey. Called *çiğ köfte* in Turkish, they are pounded and traditionally flavoured with approximately 30 different spices before being served individually in the cup of a small lettuce leaf with a wedge of lemon to squeeze over them.

150 g/1 cup minus 1 tablespoon
   fine bulgur
225 g/8 oz. lean beef, finely
   minced/ground
1 onion, very finely chopped
2–3 garlic cloves, crushed
1 tablespoon tomato purée/paste
2 teaspoons finely chopped dried
   red chilli/chile, or paprika
2 teaspoons ground cumin
1 teaspoon ground coriander
1 teaspoon ground cinnamon
1 teaspoon ground allspice
½ teaspoon ground fenugreek
sea salt and freshly ground
   black pepper
small bunch of fresh flat-leaf parsley,
   very finely chopped

To serve:
1 Cos/Romaine lettuce, or 2 little
   gem lettuces
2 lemons, cut into wedges
2 fresh green chillies/chiles, deseeded
   and finely sliced, lengthways
a bunch of fresh flat-leaf
   parsley leaves

Serves 4-6

Rinse and drain the bulgur, tip it into a bowl, and pour in just enough boiling water to cover it. Leave the bulgur to plump up for 10–15 minutes, then drain it thoroughly and squeeze it dry with your hands.

Put the minced/ground beef and bulgur into a bowl and knead it together. Add the onion, garlic, tomato purée/paste and spices, and knead well for about 5 minutes. Season with salt and pepper, add the parsley, and continue to knead for another 4–5 minutes, lifting the mixture into the air and slapping it down into the base of the bowl.

Arrange the lettuce leaves on a serving plate. Divide the mixture into small balls, press each one flat in the palm of your hand, pinch it between your thumb and forefinger to form a couple of indentations for the lemon juice, and arrange them on the lettuce leaves.

Serve the tartare patties with the lemon wedges, sliced chillies/chiles, and the parsley leaves to chew on to cut the spice. Pick up a lettuce-leaf parcel in your hand, squeeze the lemon juice into the indentation, and pop the whole thing into your mouth.

Pickled cabbage rolls filled with walnuts, garlic and chillies

Pickles are eaten much more frequently in the Middle Eastern region than anywhere else. A little dish of pickles is nearly always included in a mezze spread, but they are also eaten on their own at any time of day, and the pickling juice is drunk to quench the thirst. There are pickle shops and pickle stalls, both with shelves stacked to the brim with jars stuffed full of every combination you can think of, such as unripe apricots and almonds, stuffed baby aubergines/eggplants, fiery hot chillies/chiles, vine leaves, and these cabbage rolls.

8 large, tender white or green
   cabbage leaves
4 garlic cloves
sea salt
225 g/2 cups shelled walnuts,
   coarsely chopped
1 fresh chilli/chile, deseeded and
   finely chopped
1 tablespoon olive oil, plus more
   to serve
300 ml/1¼ cups cider vinegar or
   white wine vinegar

Serves 4

Place the cabbage leaves in a steamer set over boiling water for 3–4 minutes to soften. Refresh under running cold water and drain well. Place the leaves on a flat surface and trim the central ribs, so that the leaves lie flat.

Using a pestle and mortar, pound the garlic with a little salt until creamy. Add the walnuts and pound to a gritty paste. Beat in the chilli/chile and bind the mixture with the oil.

Place a spoonful of the mixture near the top of each leaf. Pull the top edge over the mixture, tuck in the sides and roll the leaf into a tight log. Place the stuffed leaves in a bowl or jar, tightly packed, and pour over the vinegar. Cover the bowl with cling film/plastic wrap, or seal the jar, and leave the stuffed cabbage parcels to marinade for at least a week.

When serving, arrange the stuffed leaves on a plate and drizzle them with a little olive oil.

Purple pickled turnips

Pickled turnips, either sliced or kept whole, a very popular because they are invariably preserved with a slice or two of beetroot/beet, which colours them purple. A source of great pride and joy, purple pickles often appear with other mezze dishes just because of their rich colour. Whenever I'm offered them, they never cease to make me smile.

8 small white turnips

4 garlic cloves, peeled

2 slices peeled beetroot/beet

300 ml/1¼ cups white wine vinegar
    or cider vinegar

300 ml/1¼ cups water

1 teaspoon sea salt

sterilized preserving jar

Trim and peel the turnips, rinse, pat dry and pop them into a sterilized jar with the garlic and beetroot/beet slices. Mix together the vinegar and water with the salt and pour the liquid over the turnips and beetroot/beet. Seal the jar with a tight-fitting, vinegar-proof lid and store for 1–2 weeks, until the turnips have taken on a purplish-pink hue. They will keep for 4–6 weeks in the fridge.

Onion, tomato and chilli relish

For an ultimate burst of savoury freshness, this relish of finely chopped vegetables is ideal. Favoured in kebab/kabob houses, this dish makes a tasty mezze dish served with pieces of toasted pitta bread.

2 large tomatoes, skinned
    (see page 51), deseeded,
    and finely chopped

2 long, green peppers, or
    1 green (bell) pepper, with
    stalk and seeds removed,
    and finely chopped

1 red or golden onion,
    finely chopped

1 fresh green chilli/chile, with
    stalk and seeds removed,
    and finely chopped

a small bunch of fresh flat-leaf
    parsley, finely chopped

a few fresh mint leaves,
    finely chopped

1 tablespoon olive oil

sea salt and freshly ground
    black pepper

Serves 4

In a bowl, mix all the finely chopped ingredients together. Bind together with the olive oil and season with salt and pepper. Spoon the mixture onto a serving dish, or into individual bowls.

FROM LEFT TO RIGHT:
Pickled cabbage rolls filled
with walnuts, garlic and
chillies; Purple pickled
turnips; Onion, tomato
and chilli relish.

DIPS

Tahini and lemon dip with parsley

Quick and easy, this popular dip is often served with warm crusty bread. It is enjoyed as a mezze dish as well as a sauce for falafel and roasted, grilled or fried vegetables and shellfish.

150 g/½ cup plus 2
  tablespoons light or dark
  tahini
freshly squeezed juice of
  2 lemons
2 garlic cloves, crushed
small bunch of fresh flat-leaf
  parsley, finely chopped

1–2 tablespoons
  pomegranate seeds
warm bread, to serve
carrot, celery or (bell) pepper,
  sliced thinly, to serve

Serves 4

In a bowl, beat the tahini until smooth. Gradually beat in the lemon juice – the mixture will thicken at first and then loosen – and add several teaspoons of cold water to lighten the mixture until it is the consistency of double/heavy cream.

Add the garlic and season the dip well with salt and pepper. Stir in most of the parsley and spoon the mixture into a serving bowl. Garnish with the rest of the parsley and a sprinkling of pomegranate seeds. Serve with warm bread, or with thin strips of celery, carrot or (bell) pepper.

Carrot and caraway purée with yogurt

Served in a mound with a hollow in the middle for a glug of delectable, creamy, garlicky yogurt, this is a favourite on our family mezze table.

900 g/2 lbs. carrots, peeled
  and thickly sliced
50 ml/3 tablespoons olive oil,
  plus extra for drizzling
freshly squeezed juice of
  1 lemon
1–2 teaspoons caraway seeds
2–3 garlic cloves, crushed

350 g/scant 1½ cups thick,
  creamy yogurt
a few fresh mint or dill leaves,
  finely chopped
fresh crusty bread, to serve

Serves 4–6

Steam the carrots until very soft. While still warm, mash them in a bowl or whizz them in an electric blender to form a smooth purée. Gradually beat in the olive oil and add the lemon juice and caraway seeds. Season the mixture well with salt and pepper.

In a bowl, beat the garlic into the yogurt and season it with salt or pepper. Spoon the warm carrot purée in a mound onto a serving dish and hollow out the middle. Spoon the yogurt into the hollow, drizzle a little olive oil over the top, and garnish with mint or dill, or both. Serve with chunks of fresh crusty bread to scoop up the carrot purée and yogurt together.

Roasted red pepper and walnut dip

I have been eating this well-travelled dip, called 'muhammara' in Arabic and Turkish, since my childhood in East Africa as you find versions of it wherever the Arab traders sailed.

3 red (bell) peppers
2 fresh red chillies/chiles
4–6 garlic cloves
150 ml/⅔ cup olive oil
150 g/1 cup walnuts, shelled
3 heaped tablespoons white
    breadcrumbs
2 tablespoons pomegranate molasses
freshly squeezed juice of 1 lemon
2 teaspoons runny honey
1–2 teaspoons ground cumin
a small bunch of fresh flat-leaf
    parsley, finely chopped
sea salt

Serves 4-6

Preheat the oven to 200°C(400°F) Gas 6.

Put the (bell) peppers into an oven dish with the chillies/chiles and garlic cloves, drizzle with half the olive oil, and put them in the preheated oven to roast for about 1 hour. Turn the peppers and chillies/chiles from time to time in the oil until the skins are slightly burnt and buckled. Remove the chillies/chiles and garlic when they are ready but leave the peppers for the full hour or longer.

Put the walnuts on a baking sheet and place them in the oven for the last 10 minutes of the cooking time, so that they are lightly toasted and emitting a nutty aroma.

Carefully peel the skins off the peppers, chillies/chiles, and garlic and remove any seeds. Roughly chop the flesh and put it into a food processer with the walnuts, breadcrumbs, pomegranate molasses, lemon juice, honey and cumin. Pour in the roasting oil and whizz to a purée. Drizzle in the rest of the oil whilst whizzing, add most of the parsley, and season well with salt.

Tip the mixture into a serving bowl, swirl a little pomegranate molasses over the top and sprinkle with the rest of the parsley. Serve with strips of toasted flatbread.

Feta, grilled pepper and chilli dip with honey

The Greeks have a great tradition of marrying salty feta with honey in a number of dishes, some of which are mirrored in Turkey and in Morocco. In Greece, the dish is known as 'htipiti'.

1 red, orange or yellow (bell) pepper
200 g/7 oz. feta
2–3 tablespoons olive oil
freshly squeezed juice of 1 lemon
1 teaspoon finely chopped dried red
    chilli/hot red pepper flakes
small bunch flat-leaf parsley, finely
    chopped
small bunch fresh mint, finely chopped
1–2 tablespoons runny honey
toasted flatbread, to serve

Serves 4

Place the pepper directly over a gas flame, under the grill, or over a charcoal grill/broiler, turning from time to time, until it is charred all over. Carefully pop the pepper into a clean resealable plastic bag to sweat for 5 minutes, then hold it under running cold water and peel off the skin. Squeeze out the excess water, cut off the stalk, and remove the seeds.

Using a pestle and mortar, or a food processor, pound the pepper to a pulp with the feta. Add the oil, lemon juice and dried chilli/hot red pepper flakes. Gently beat in most of the parsley and mint and spoon the mixture into serving bowl.

Heat the honey in a small pot and drizzle it over the dip. Garnish with the rest of the parsley and mint and serve with toasted flatbread.

Smoked aubergine dip with tahini and parsley

This classic smoked aubergine/eggplant dish is commonly known as *baba ghanoush* or *moutabal* in the eastern Mediterranean region. There are endless variations involving yogurt, different herbs, chopped nuts, feta and crushed chickpeas, but my favourite version, which I would just like to squeeze in here as an alternative, is the Turkish combination of smoked aubergine/eggplant flesh mixed with 2 tablespoons olive oil, the juice of 1 lemon, 2 crushed garlic cloves, 4–5 tablespoons or more of thick, creamy yogurt, and seasoned well with salt. The aubergines/eggplants can be smoked directly on the gas flame or over a charcoal grill – the latter is less messy as the skin of the aubergine/eggplant toughens so you just slit it open to scoop out the warm flesh. The strong smoky flavour is essential to this dish, so you can't cheat by baking the aubergines/eggplants.

2–3 medium-sized
    aubergines/eggplants
2–3 tablespoons tahini
freshly squeezed juice of 1 lemon
2–3 tablespoons pomegranate
    molasses/syrup
2 garlic cloves, crushed
a small bunch of fresh flat-leaf
    parsley, finely chopped (reserve
    a little for the garnish)
sea salt and freshly ground
    black pepper
olive oil, for drizzling
1 tablespoon fresh pomegranate seeds
warm crusty bread or toasted
    flatbread, to serve

Serves 4–6

Place the aubergines/eggplants directly over a gas flame, or over a charcoal grill. Use tongs to turn them from time to time, until they are soft to touch and the skin is charred and flaky. Place them in a clean resealable plastic bag for a minute to sweat and, when cool enough to handle, hold them by the stems under cold running water and peel off the skin. Squeeze out the excess water and place the flesh on a chopping board. (If using a charcoal grill, the skin toughens instead of charring, so it is easier to slit the aubergine/eggplant open like a canoe and scoop out the softened flesh). Chop the flesh to a pulp.

In a bowl, beat the aubergine/eggplant pulp with the tahini, lemon juice, and pomegranate molasses to a creamy paste. Add the garlic and parsley and season well with salt and pepper – adjust the flavour according to taste by adding more lemon juice, pomegranate molasses/syrup or salt.

Beat the mixture thoroughly and tip it into a serving bowl. Drizzle a little olive oil over the top to keep it moist and garnish with the reserved parsley and pomegranate seeds. Serve with chunks of warm, crusty bread.

FOLLOWING PAGES, FROM LEFT TO RIGHT: Labna with deep-fried carrots and dill; Labna with saffron, apricots and pistachios; Labna with harissa, coriander and honey; Labna with roasted beetroot and pine nuts; Labna with dried and fresh mint.

Labna with dried and fresh mint

This fresh, strong-flavoured Turkish dip ('haydari') is ideal in the summer with a warm crusty loaf.

500 g/2 cups Labna (see page 20)
2–3 garlic cloves, crushed
1 tablespoon dried mint
sea salt and freshly ground black pepper
small bunch fresh mint leaves,
  finely chopped
a drizzle of olive oil

In a bowl, beat the Labna with the crushed garlic. Add the dried mint and season well with salt and pepper. Fold in the fresh mint and spoon the mixture into a serving bowl.

Drizzle a little olive oil over the dip and sprinkle with the reserved fresh mint. Serve with strips of toasted pitta bread.

Labna with harissa, coriander and honey

I created this dip for my cookery workshops to make with our own fresh yogurt cheese and Harissa.

500 g/2 cups Labna (see page 20)
2 garlic cloves, crushed
½ teaspoon sea salt
2 teaspoons Harissa (see page 12)
a small bunch fresh coriander/
  cilantro, finely chopped, plus
  extra for garnishing
1 tablespoon runny honey

Beat the Labna in a bowl with the garlic and salt and stir in the Harissa – taste the mixture to get the right quantity of Harissa to suit your palate. Adjust the seasoning with more salt if necessary and beat in the coriander/cilantro.

Spoon the mixture into a serving bowl and drizzle the honey over the top. Garnish with a sprinkling of coriander/cilantro and serve with strips of crusty or toasted pitta bread, or a selection of crudités.

Labna with deep-fried carrots and dill

This is my favourite version of the popular carrot tzatziki, which we often tuck into at home.

2–3 carrots
sunflower oil, for deep-frying
500 g/2 cups Labna (see page 20)
2–3 garlic cloves, crushed
sea salt and freshly ground black pepper
small bunch fresh dill, finely chopped,
  plus extra for garnishing
a drizzle of olive oil

Peel the carrots, cut them into quarters lengthways, and slice them finely. Heat enough oil for deep-frying in the base of a small frying pan/skillet or wok and fry the carrots in batches until they are lightly golden brown in colour. Drain them on paper towels.

Beat the Labna in a bowl with the garlic and season well with the salt and pepper. Add the dill and fold in most of the carrots while they are still warm.

Spoon the mixture onto a serving dish and scatter the remainder of the carrots over and around them. Drizzle a little olive oil over the top and garnish with the rest of the dill. Serve with strips of toasted pitta bread.

Labna with saffron, apricots and pistachios

Sweet, lemony and bright, this dip lands somewhere in between savoury and sweet mezze and could be served as either. Variations of this dip are enjoyed in Iran, Turkey and Syria, and it is usually served with strips of toasted flatbread as part of a mezze spread, or as a dish on its own.

a pinch of saffron fronds
2–3 teaspoons freshly squeezed
lemon juice
500 g/2 cups Labna (see page 20)
1–2 garlic cloves, crushed
sea salt and freshly ground
black pepper
125 g/1 cup dried apricots,
finely chopped
1 tablespoon olive oil
1 tablespoon shelled roasted
pistachios, coarsely ground

Put the saffron fronds in a small dish and stir in the lemon juice. Leave the fronds to steep in the juice for 10 minutes to weep their dye.

In a bowl, beat the Labna with the garlic and season well with salt and pepper. Fold in the apricots and drizzle in the saffron fronds and lemon juice so that it forms streaks through dip – you can reserve a splash of the yellow juice to mix with the olive oil for the top if you like.

Spoon the mixture into a serving bowl, drizzle with a little olive oil, and sprinkle the ground pistachios over the top. Serve the dip with strips of toasted pitta bread.

Labna with roasted beetroot and pine nuts

This winter dip is a delicious pinky-purple version of the well-known Greek tzatziki made with grated cucumber. To retain the natural sweetness and firm texture, it is best to steam or roast the beetroot/beet.

2 medium-sized beetroot/beet
2 tablespoons olive oil
sea salt and freshly ground
black pepper
500 g/2 cups Labna (see page 20)
2–3 garlic cloves, crushed
1 tablespoon pine nuts
1 tablespoon butter
a scant teaspoon finely chopped
dried chilli/hot red pepper flakes
1 teaspoon dried oregano

All dips serve 4

Preheat the oven to 180°C (360°F) Gas 4.

Place the whole beetroot/beet in the middle of a piece of aluminum foil lining a small oven dish. Drizzle 1 tablespoon olive oil over them, sprinkle with salt, pull up the sides of the foil to enclose the beetroot/beet in a package, and pop them in the preheated oven for about 1½ hours.

Remove the beetroot/beet from the foil package and, when they are cool enough to handle, peel off the skins and grate them on the widest teeth on the grater.

Beat the labna in a bowl with the garlic and season well with salt and pepper. Fold in the grated beetroot/beet (reserve a little for garnishing) and tip the mixture onto a serving dish. Garnish with the reserved beetroot/beet.

Dry roast the pine nuts in a frying pan/skillet until they emit a nutty aroma and turn golden brown, then stir in the butter until it melts. Add the finely chopped chilli/hot red pepper flakes and drizzle the mixture over the dip. Scatter the oregano over the top and serve with strips of toasted pitta bread.

SALADS & STUFFED VEGETABLES

Smoked aubergine salad with grilled peppers, spring onions and parsley

Aubergines/eggplants play a huge role on the mezze table – there are reputed to be around 200 dishes made with them – and smoking them over a gas flame, or on a charcoal grill, is one of the most enjoyable ways of cooking and eating them. The soft, smoky-flavoured flesh is combined with other ingredients for a variety of mezze dishes, such as the well-known Lebanese and Syrian specialty, baba ghanoush (see page 38). This recipe is a popular salad all over the Mediterranean region and is one of my favourite aubergine/eggplant mezze dishes.

2–3 large aubergines/eggplants
2 red (bell) peppers
2–3 garlic cloves, crushed
3–4 spring onions/scallions, trimmed and finely sliced
a bunch of fresh flat-leaf parsley, coarsely chopped
sea salt and freshly ground black pepper
2–3 tablespoons olive oil
2 tablespoons pomegranate syrup/molasses, or the freshly squeezed juice of 1 lemon

Serves 4-6

Place the aubergines/eggplants and (bell) peppers directly on the gas flame, or on the grid over a charcoal grill. Over the flame, the skins of the aubergines/eggplants and peppers will buckle and flake a little and will make a bit of a mess of your gas cooker but, over the charcoal grill, the skins will toughen and brown, leaving no mess! It doesn't matter which method you choose, but you are looking for the flesh of both the aubergines/eggplants and the peppers to soften, so you need to keep turning them to make sure they are evenly smoked. Once soft, pop them both into a clean, resealable plastic bag to sweat for 5 minutes, then hold them by the stalks under cold running water and peel off the skins. Squeeze out the excess water and put them on a chopping board. Remove the stalks of the aubergines/eggplants and chop the flesh to a coarse pulp. Remove the stalks and seeds of the peppers and chop the flesh to a coarse pulp as well.

Tip the pulped flesh into a bowl and add the garlic, spring onions/scallions and parsley. Season well with salt and pepper (the smoked aubergine/eggplant flesh needs salt to bring out the flavour) and bind the salad with the olive oil and pomegranate syrup/molasses or lemon juice. Drizzle a little extra pomegranate syrup/molasses over the top before serving.

Pomegranate salad with basil

From Iran to Morocco, variations of this refreshing, crunchy salad appear on the tables of the fertile fruit-growing regions. The ancient pomegranate is cherished for its medicinal properties, its jewel-like seeds symbolic of fertility and prosperity, and its role in many myths and legends.

1 white onion
1 teaspoon sea salt
6 fresh pomegranates
3–4 tablespoons pomegranate syrup/molasses
a small bunch of fresh basil leaves, shredded

Serves 4-6

Slice the onion in half lengthways, then slice the two halves in half again crossways. Using the grain of the onion as a guide, finely slice the quarters into thin, bite-sized strips. Scatter the strips of onion on a plate, sprinkle with the salt, and put them aside to weep.

Cut the pomegranates into quarters, from the flower to the stalk end (do this on a board with a grooved perimeter if you can so that you catch the juice). Pick up one of the quarters in your hands and very carefully, using your thumbs and forefingers, flick the seeds into a bowl, leaving as much of the pith and membrane behind as you can. Once you have flicked the seeds of all the quarters, pick out any bits of pith that have landed in the salad and any seeds that don't look fresh and juicy, so that you have a bowl of gleaming seeds that look like precious jewels.

Tip the onions into a colander and rinse off all the salt. Drain them on several layers of thick paper towels and pat dry. Add the onions to the pomegranate seeds and toss in the pomegranate syrup/molasses. Toss a few basil leaves through the salad, garnish with the rest, and serve with a selection of mezze dishes, particularly the spicier ones.

Celery and coconut salad with lime

Crunchy and creamy with a citrus burst from the fresh lime, this salad is delightfully refreshing on a hot day. It is best prepared with the juicy flesh of a fresh coconut, which, while sometimes time-consuming, is well worth the effort.

6 long celery stalks, grated (reserve the leaves for the garnish)
½ a fresh coconut, grated
zest and freshly squeezed juice of 1 lime
3–4 tablespoons thick, creamy yogurt

2 garlic cloves, crushed
sea salt and freshly ground black pepper
a few fresh mint leaves, shredded

Serves 4

Tip the grated celery and coconut into a bowl. Toss in the lime zest and juice.

Mix the yogurt and garlic and season well with salt and pepper. Tip the mixture onto the celery and coconut and mix well. Leave the salad to sit for 10–15 minutes so that the celery begins to weep a little into the yogurt.

Spoon the salad into a serving bowl, or the empty coconut shells, and garnish with the celery and mint leaves.

Orange salad with dates, chillies and preserved lemon

Attractive and refreshing, this salad epitomizes the culinary characteristics of North Africa and the Middle East – fresh, sweet, hot and salty.

4 ripe, sweet oranges
175 g/1¼ cups moist stoned/pitted
   dried dates
1–2 fresh red chillies/chiles, deseeded
   and finely sliced
peel of 1 Preserved Lemon (see page
   19), finely sliced
1 tablespoon finely chopped fresh
   coriander/cilantro
2 tablespoons orange-blossom water
1 tablespoon pomegranate
   syrup/molasses

Serves 4–6

Peel the oranges, removing as much of the pith as possible. Place the oranges on a plate to catch the juice and finely slice them into circles or half moons, removing any pips. Arrange the oranges in a shallow bowl and pour the puddle of juice over them.

Finely slice the dates lengthways and scatter them over the oranges. Scatter the sliced chillies/chiles, Preserved Lemon rind, and fresh coriander/cilantro over the top.

Splash in the orange blossom water and drizzle the pomegranate molasses over the salad. Leave the dates to soften and the flavours to mingle for 10–15 minutes. Gently toss the salad just before serving.

Parsley salad with mint and bulgur

The key to preparing this version of tabbouleh is to slice the parsley finely, rather than chop it, so that the fine strands remain dry and fresh, not mushy, and to dress it at the last minute.

60 g/⅓ cup fine bulgur
freshly squeezed juice of 2 lemons
a large bunch of fresh flat-leaf parsley
   (roughly 225 g/8 oz.), rinsed and
   shaken dry
a bunch of fresh mint leaves, rinsed
   and shaken dry
2–3 spring onions/scallions, trimmed
   and finely sliced
1–2 tablespoons olive oil
2 tablespoons pomegranate
   syrup/molasses
sea salt and freshly ground black pepper

Serves 4–6

Rinse the bulgur in cold water and drain well. Place it in a bowl and pour over the lemon juice – if you need to, add a little warm water so that there is enough liquid to just cover the bulgur. Leave it to soften for 10 minutes while you prepare the rest of the salad.

Place the parsley on a chopping board and hold the bunch tightly with one hand while you slice the leaves and the tops of the stalks as finely as you can with a sharp knife – it is important to slice or shred the parsley, not to chop it. Tip the sliced or shredded parsley into a bowl. Slice the mint leaves in the same way and add them to the bowl. Add the spring onions/scallions and the soaked bulgur.

Gently toss in the oil and pomegranate molasses and season the salad with salt and pepper to taste. Spoon the salad into a serving bowl, or, alternatively, line a dish with lettuce or endive leaves and tip the salad in the middle so that you can use the leaves to scoop it up.

Toasted bread and parsley salad with pomegranate molasses and sumac

No mezze table is complete without a salad of fresh of tomatoes, peppers and onion. The addition of toasted bread transforms the salad into a Lebanese and Syrian classic called 'fattoush'.

2 pitta breads or 3 slices of crusty loaf, toasted and broken into bite-sized pieces
3 tablespoons olive oil
freshly squeezed juice of ½ a lemon
½ Cos/Romaine lettuce, trimmed and chopped
2–3 tomatoes, skinned, deseeded and chopped
1 red or green (bell) pepper, deseeded and finely sliced
1 red onion, halved lengthways and halved again crossways, and finely sliced
a big bunch of fresh flat-leaf parsley, coarsely chopped
2–3 tablespoons pomegranate syrup/molasses
2 teaspoons ground sumac
sea salt and freshly ground black pepper

Serves 4–6

Put all the broken pieces of toasted bread into a bowl and toss in 1–2 tablespoons olive oil and the lemon juice to soften it a little but not to make it soggy.

Place all the vegetables in a bowl and add the parsley and bread. Drizzle the rest of the olive oil and the pomegranate syrup/molasses over the salad and sprinkle with the sumac. Season with salt (commercial sumac is sometimes combined with salt so check the taste) and pepper and toss the salad just before serving.

Walnut, parsley and chilli salad with pomegranate molasses

Regarded as the king of nuts, walnuts play a big role in the savoury and sweet dishes of the region and they make this simple salad quite special. I first enjoyed this mezze dish in a Kurdish household, as it is popular in the region where the borders of Turkey, Syria and Iraq meet.

225 g/generous 1½ cups walnuts
a large bunch of fresh flat-leaf parsley
2 fresh green chillies/chiles, deseeded and finely chopped
1 red onion, finely chopped
1 teaspoon sea salt
2 tomatoes
2–3 tablespoons pomegranate syrup/molasses

Serves 4–6

Chop the walnuts – not too fine, not too coarse, so that they have a bite to them – and tip them into a shallow serving bowl. Chop the parsley leaves and stalks – again not too fine, not too coarse – and add them to the bowl with the chillies/chiles and the onion. Sprinkle the salt over the chopped onion and leave it to weep a little. Don't toss the salad at this stage.

Meanwhile, scald the tomatoes in a pan of boiling water for 2–3 seconds, drain and refresh under running cold water to loosen the skins. Peel and quarter the tomatoes, scoop out the seeds, chop the tomato flesh to a similar size as the parsley and walnuts, and add them to the bowl. Drizzle the pomegranate syrup/molasses over the salad and toss it gently before serving.

Chicken salad with walnuts, melted chilli butter and coriander

This creamy, tasty chicken salad is of Circassian origin. The Ottoman version, called 'çerkez tavuğu' in Turkish, involves pouring melted chilli butter over the top. Other versions (which stretch from places as far and wide as eastern Anatolia, Armenia, Azerbaijan and Iran), include threads of fresh coriander/cilantro tossed through the salad. As I like the chilli butter and the coriander/cilantro, I have included both in this recipe.

1 medium-sized, free-range
   chicken, trimmed of
   excess fat
3 slices day-old white bread,
   with crusts removed
150 ml/⅔ cup whole milk
225 g/generous 1½ cups
   walnuts (reserve 1
   tablespoonful for
   garnishing)
4–6 garlic cloves
sea salt and freshly ground
   black pepper
25 g/2 tablespoons butter
1 teaspoon finely chopped
   dried red chilli/hot red
   pepper flakes

a small bunch of fresh
   coriander/cilantro leaves,
   finely chopped

For the stock:
1 onion, quartered
1 carrot, peeled and chopped
2 celery sticks, chopped
4–6 cloves
4–6 allspice berries
4–6 black peppercorns
1 teaspoon coriander seeds
2 fresh bay leaves and a small
   bunch of flat-leaf parsley
   stalks, bruised and tied
   together

Serves 6-8

Put all the stock ingredients into a deep pot with the chicken. Pour in enough water to just cover the chicken, bring it to the boil, then reduce the heat and cover the pot. Simmer for about 1 hour until the chicken is very tender.

Remove the chicken from the pot and leave it until cool enough to handle. Meanwhile, boil up the stock with the lid off for about 15 minutes to reduce it. Strain the stock and season it with salt and pepper. When the chicken has cooled a little, pull off the skin and discard it, then tear all the chicken meat into thin strips and put them into a bowl.

In a shallow bowl, soak the bread in the milk. Using a pestle and mortar, pound the walnuts with the garlic to form a paste, or whizz them together in an electric blender. Beat in the soaked bread to form a creamy sauce and add it to the chicken. Using a ladle, add enough of the warm, seasoned stock to bind the chicken with the walnut and bread sauce, until it is light and creamy.

Arrange the chicken salad in a mound on serving dish. Just before serving, roughly chop the reserved walnuts and roast for 1 minute in a small saucepan, until they emit a nutty aroma. Add the butter until it melts and begins to froth and stir in the chilli/hot red pepper flakes. Pour the melted butter mixture over the chicken and garnish with the chopped coriander/cilantro.

Gypsy salad with feta, chillies and dried mint

This salad is really called 'gypsy rice', as the crumbled feta is supposed to represent grains of rice, which in the past would have been too expensive to buy on a regular basis. It is a variation on the theme of shepherd and harvest salads, usually consisting of daily market vegetables common to the Mediterranean region, such as tomatoes, (bell) peppers and onions.

2 red onions, cut in half lengthways and finely sliced along the grain

1 teaspoon sea salt

2 red (bell) peppers, deseeded and sliced

2 green chillies/chiles, halved lengthways, deseeded and finely sliced

2–3 garlic cloves, finely chopped

2 tablespoons olive oil

2 tablespoons pomegranate syrup/molasses, or the freshly squeezed juice of 1 lemon

225 g/8 oz. feta, rinsed and crumbled or grated

2 teaspoons dried mint

1 teaspoon ground sumac

Serves 4-6

Sprinkle the onions with the salt to draw out the juice for 5–10 minutes. Rinse and pat dry.

Put the onions, (bell) peppers and chillies/chiles into a shallow bowl with the garlic. Add the oil and pomegranate syrup/molasses or lemon juice and scatter the feta over the top. Sprinkle with the mint and sumac and gently toss just before serving.

Bean salad with red onions, eggs, olives and anchovies

Beans play an important role in the staple diet of the Middle East and they are a traditional addition to any mezze table in the form of salads, puréed dips and savoury balls. There are also several cooked bean dishes, which are served cold as mezze. The most popular beans for mezze are the dried haricot/navy, borlotti, and black-eyed varieties as well as broad/fava beans, both fresh and dried. This particular salad is usually prepared with haricot/navy or Egyptian brown beans.

225 g/1¼ cups dried haricot/navy beans, soaked in plenty of water overnight

1 red onion, cut in half lengthways, then in half crossways, and sliced with the grain

3 tablespoons black olives, drained

a bunch of fresh flat-leaf parsley, roughly chopped

4 tablespoons olive oil

freshly squeezed juice of 1 lemon

sea salt and freshly ground black pepper

3 eggs, boiled to just firm, shelled and quartered

12 preserved anchovy fillets, rinsed and drained

lemon wedges, to serve

Serves 4-6

Drain the soaked beans and tip them into a pan with plenty of water. Bring the water to the boil, reduce the heat and simmer for about 45 minutes, until the beans are cooked but still firm, with a bite to them, not soft and mushy. Drain the beans, rinse well under cold water and pick out any loose skins.

Tip the beans into a wide shallow bowl. Add the onion, olives, and most of the parsley. Toss in the olive oil and lemon juice, and season to taste with salt and pepper. Place the quartered eggs and anchovy fillets on top and scatter with the remaining parsley. Serve with wedges of lemon to squeeze over the beans.

Artichokes with broad beans and almonds

Fresh globe artichokes should be treated like flowers and stood in a jug/pitcher of water until ready to use. In the early summer, the markets and street-sellers of the eastern Mediterranean region display crates of artichokes, which they skilfully prepare for you on the spot. Frozen ready-prepared artichoke bottoms are also available in some supermarkets and Middle Eastern stores. However, you can prepare your own: pull off the outer leaves and cut off the stalks; using a sharp knife, slice away the purple choke, the small leaves and any hard bits; remove any fibres with the edge of a spoon and rub the artichoke bottoms with a mixture of lemon juice and salt to prevent them from discolouring.

175 g/1½ cups fresh broad/fava beans, shelled
4 fresh globe artichokes, trimmed to their bottoms (see above)
125 ml/¾ cup plus 1 tablespoon olive oil
freshly squeezed juice of 1 lemon
50 ml/3 tablespoons water
2 teaspoons granulated sugar
sea salt
90 g/1 scant cup blanched almonds
a small bunch of dill, chopped

Serves 4

Place the broad/fava beans in pot of water and bring it to the boil. Reduce the heat and simmer the beans for about 40 minutes, until tender. Drain and refresh under running cold water. Remove the skins and put the beans aside.

Place the artichoke bottoms in heavy-based saucepan. Mix together the olive oil, lemon juice and water and pour it over the artichokes. Cover the pan with a lid and poach the artichokes gently for about 20 minutes. Add the sugar, a little salt, beans and almonds and continue to poach gently for a further 10 minutes, until the artichokes are tender. Toss in half the dill and turn off the heat. Leave the artichokes to cool in the saucepan.

Lift the artichoke bottoms out of the saucepan and place them, hollow-side up, on a serving dish. Spoon the beans and almonds into the middle of the artichokes and around them. Garnish with the rest of the dill and serve at room temperature.

Vine leaves stuffed with aromatic rice

My favourite version of this popular mezze dish is one that I enjoyed at the home of an Iranian friend who rolled the stuffed leaves into long, thin fingers and served them at room temperature with hot melted butter. The dish works well with both fresh and preserved vine leaves (see below).

12–16 fresh or preserved vine leaves (see below), plus a few extra to line the pot
1–2 tablespoons olive oil
1 onion, finely chopped
2 garlic cloves, finely chopped
1 tablespoon pine nuts
1 tablespoon tiny currants, soaked in boiling water for 10 minutes and drained
1 teaspoon ground allspice
1 teaspoon ground cinnamon
150 g/¾ cup short-grain or risotto rice, well rinsed and drained
sea salt and freshly ground black pepper
a small bunch of fresh flat-leaf parsley, finely chopped
a small bunch of fresh dill, finely chopped
a small bunch of fresh mint, finely chopped

For the cooking liquid:
100 ml/⅔ cup olive oil
100 ml/7 tablespoons water
freshly squeezed juice of 1 lemon
1 teaspoon granulated sugar

For serving:
2 lemons, cut into wedges

Serves 4

Prepare the vine leaves (see below) and drain thoroughly. Stack them on a plate, cover with a clean, damp tea/dish towel to keep them moist, and put aside.

Heat the oil in a heavy-based pot and stir in the onion and garlic, until they begin to colour. Stir in the pine nuts for 1–2 minutes, until they turn golden. Add the currants and when they plump up, stir in the spices. Toss in the rice, making sure it is coated in the spices, and pour in enough water to just cover the rice. Season with salt and pepper and bring the water to the boil. Reduce the heat and cook for about 10 minutes until all the water has been absorbed and the rice is still firm. Toss in the fresh herbs and leave the rice to cool.

Place a vine leaf on a plate or board and put a heaped teaspoon of rice at the bottom of the leaf, where the stem would have been. Fold the stem edge over the filling, then fold both of the side edges in towards the middle of the leaf, so that the filling is sealed in. Now roll the leaf up like a small fat cigar. If you prefer, place the rice in a thin line along the stem edge, and you'll then be able to roll the leaf into long, thin finger. Place the stuffed vine leaf in the palm of your hand and squeeze it lightly to fix the shape. Put aside and repeat with the remaining leaves.

In a small bowl, mix together the cooking liquid ingredients. Line the bottom of a shallow pan with the extra vine leaves, then place the stuffed vine leaves on top, tightly packed side by side. Pour the olive oil mixture over the stuffed vine leaves and place a plate on top of them to prevent them from unravelling during cooking. Cover the pan and simmer gently for about 1 hour, topping up the cooking liquid if necessary. Leave the stuffed vine leaves to cool in the pan, then lift them out, arrange on a plate and serve with lemon wedges.

Preparing the vine leaves

To prepare fresh vine leaves, bring a large pot of water to the boil and plunge the leaves into it for 1–2 minutes so that they soften. Drain and refresh them under running cold water, making sure they are thoroughly drained before using. Trim off the stems and keep them covered in the refrigerator for 2–3 days.

To prepare preserved vine leaves, place them in a deep bowl and pour boiling water over them. Leave them to soak for 15–20 minutes, using a fork to gently separate the leaves. Drain the leaves and put them back in the bowl with cold water. Leave them to soak for 2–3 minutes to get rid of any salty residue, then drain them thoroughly.

Aubergines stuffed with onions, tomatoes and herbs

Whether the Imam fainted from shock or pleasure as a result of the quantity of olive oil used in this dish, no one knows, but the 'Imam fainted' is the translation of this Ottoman classic, 'imam bayıldı'. Olive oil plays a central role in a number of Ottoman vegetable dishes, which are cooked in the oil for flavour and are always served cold. These deliciously tender aubergines/eggplants can be filled and baked in the oven or, following the more traditional method, gently poached.

4 medium-sized
    aubergines/eggplants
sunflower oil
2 onions, halved lengthways and
    finely sliced
4 tomatoes, skinned (see page 51),
    deseeded and roughly chopped
2–3 garlic cloves, finely chopped
a bunch of flat-leaf parsley,
    finely chopped (reserve a little
    for garnishing)
bunch fresh dill, finely chopped
    (reserve a little for garnishing)
1 teaspoon salt
150 ml/1 ⅓ cups olive oil
50 ml/3 tablespoons water
freshly squeezed juice of 1 lemon
1 tablespoon granulated sugar

Serves 4

Using a sharp knife or a potato peeler, peel the aubergines/eggplants in stripes like a zebra. Place them in a bowl of salted water for 5 minutes, then pat them dry. Heat up enough sunflower oil for frying in a frying pan/skillet. Place the aubergines/eggplants in the oil and fry for 2–3 minutes, rolling them over in the oil, to soften and lightly brown them – the oil will spit, so have a lid at hand.

Transfer the softened aubergines/eggplants to a wide, shallow pan, placing them side by side, and slit them open, keeping the ends and bottom intact, so that they resemble hollowed-out canoes.

In a bowl, mix together the onions, tomatoes, garlic and herbs. Add the salt and a little of the olive oil. Spoon the onion and tomato mixture into the aubergine/eggplant pockets, packing it in tightly, so that all of it is used up. Mix together the rest of the olive oil with the water and lemon juice, pour it over the aubergines/eggplants, and sprinkle the sugar over the top.

Cover the pan with a lid and place it over a medium heat to get the oil hot and create some steam. Reduce the heat and cook the aubergines/eggplants gently for about 40 minutes, basting them from time to time, until they are soft and tender and only a little oil is left in the bottom of the pan. Leave them to cool in the pan.

Carefully lift the stuffed aubergines/eggplants onto a serving dish and spoon the little bit of oil left in the pan over them. Garnish with the reserved dill and parsley and serve at room temperature with wedges of lemon to squeeze over them.

Baked stuffed bell peppers in olive oil

Peppers, aubergines/eggplants, courgettes/zucchini, apples and apricots are some of the fruits and vegetables cooked and stuffed in this manner and served as a mezze dish. Generally the aromatic rice filling is the same for all them and they are cooked in olive oil and served cold. The peppers used for this dish in Turkey and Lebanon are usually small and green, and the opening is sealed with a red tomato cap for colour. I like to use red, orange, and yellow (bell) peppers, as they are sweeter than the green ones and, for colour, I cap them with each other's stalk ends.

Preheat the oven to 180°C (360°F) Gas 4.

For the rice, heat the olive oil in a heavy-based frying pan/skillet and stir in the onion and sugar for 1–2 minutes, then stir in the pine nuts until they turn golden. Stir in the currants until they plump up, then add the cinnamon, allspice, dried mint and tomato purée/paste and stir in the rice, making sure it is coated in the mixture.

Pour in 400 ml/1⅔ cups water, season with a little salt and pepper, and bring it to the boil. Reduce the heat and cook gently for about 15 minutes, until the water has been absorbed but the rice is still firm. Toss in the fresh herbs.

Slice the stalk end off each pepper neatly and remove the core and seeds. Keep the trimmed stalk ends as lids and rinse the peppers. Fill the peppers with the rice mixture and place them side by side, so that they prop each other up, in a shallow baking dish. Pop on the lids, alternating the colours.

In a bowl, mix together the olive oil and lemon juice with 50 ml/3 tablespoons water and the sugar. Pour the mixture over and around the peppers and pop them in the preheated oven for about 50 minutes, basting from time to time, until they are tender and the cooking liquid is a little caramelized. Leave the peppers to cool in the cooking liquid then transfer them to a serving dish. Spoon some of the caramelized liquid over them and drizzle a little pomegranate syrup/molasses over the top.

4 colourful (bell) peppers
50 ml/3 tablespoons olive oil
freshly squeezed juice of 1 lemon
2 teaspoons granulated sugar
pomegranate syrup/molasses,
　for drizzling
lemon wedges, to serve

For the rice stuffing:
2–3 tablespoons olive oil
1 red onion, finely chopped
1 teaspoon granulated sugar
2 tablespoons pine nuts
2 tablespoons tiny currants,
　soaked in boiling water for
　10 minutes and drained
2 teaspoons ground cinnamon

1 teaspoon allspice
1 teaspoon dried mint
½ teaspoon ground allspice
1 teaspoon tomato purée/paste
200 g/1 cup short-grain or
　risotto rice, washed and
　drained
sea salt and freshly ground
　black pepper
a small bunch of flat-leaf
　parsley, finely chopped
a small bunch of fresh dill,
　finely chopped
a small bunch of fresh mint,
　finely chopped

Serves 4

HOT MEZZE

When it comes to hot dishes, street food and mezze merge. If you wander around a market or a busy neighbourhood, you will come across vendors roasting chestnuts over makeshift charcoal grills or frying kibbeh, köfte, or falafel in large cauldrons. You will also come across flatbread vendors and savoury pastry stalls selling puff and flaky specialities in a variety of shapes and sizes, ranging from half moons, tiny kayaks, rolled cigars and square parcels. The aroma of grilling meat will lure you towards kebabs/kabobs of every description and the smoke and steam rising from the grills and curved pans by the harbours will reveal the day's catch.

So, the interpretation of hot mezze is flexible, as it often consists of main courses or street food in miniature. There are some dishes specifically designed to be hot mezze, such as deep-fried shellfish or vegetables, hot dips, and filled pastries, but there are also mini kebabs/kabobs, baby vegetables cooked instead of larger ones, and fried small fish. The concept is simple as long as the portions are small and, in most cases, the dishes marry well with fresh salads and dips, sweetmeats and fruit in syrup.

DIPS & PURÉES

Hot hummus with pine nuts and chilli butter

I first had this heavenly hummus some 30 years ago in a tiny village near Kars in eastern Anatolia. Taking refuge in a simple, one-roomed dwelling after a hazardous journey through PKK (Kurdistan Workers' Party) territory cloaked in darkness, the hot, creamy dip, baked in a clay dish, was as welcome as it was soothing. It was such a memorable discovery that I have been writing about it, and enthusiastically devouring it, ever since. When most people think of the word 'hummus', they think of the ubiquitous thick, smooth, chickpea purée served at room temperature with pitta bread or crudités, not this delectable, hot version, called *sıcak humus* in Turkish. I add yogurt to the traditional recipe to make it more mousse-like and utterly moreish.

2 x 400 g/14-oz. cans chickpeas,
    drained and thoroughly rinsed
2 teaspoons cumin seeds
2–3 garlic cloves, crushed
roughly 4 tablespoons olive oil
freshly squeezed juice of 2 lemons
2 tablespoons tahini
500 ml/2 cups thick, creamy yogurt
sea salt and freshly ground
    black pepper
2 tablespoons pine nuts
50 g/3 tablespoons butter
1 teaspoon finely chopped dried
    red chilli/chile
warm crusty bread, to serve

Serves 4–6

Preheat the oven to 200°C(400°F) Gas 6.

Instead of using a pestle and mortar to pound the chickpeas to a paste in the traditional manner, make life easy and tip the chickpeas into an electric blender. Add the cumin seeds, garlic, olive oil and lemon juice and whizz the mixture to a thick paste. Add the tahini and continue to blend until the mixture is really thick and smooth. Add the yogurt and whizz until the mixture has loosened a little and the texture is creamy. Season generously with salt and pepper and tip the mixture into an ovenproof dish.

Roast the pine nuts in small frying pan/skillet until they begin to brown and emit a nutty aroma. Add the butter to the pine nuts and stir until it melts. Stir in the chopped chilli/chile and pour the melted butter over the hummus, spooning the pine nuts all over the surface.

Pop the dish into the preheated oven for about 25 minutes, until the hummus has risen a little and most of the butter has been absorbed. Serve immediately with chunks of warm crusty bread.

Warm spinach with currants, pine nuts and yogurt

The Iranians, the Lebanese, the Turks and the Moroccans all have their own variations of this velvety dish of cooked spinach combined with yogurt. Served as mezze in restaurants throughout the Middle East, this is a delicious way to enjoy spinach. Pulled from several traditions, my version includes currants, onions and pine nuts, served warm with dollops of cool, garlic-flavoured yogurt and chunks of crusty bread.

500 g/1 lb. 2 oz. fresh spinach leaves,
    thoroughly washed and drained
250 ml/1 cup thick, creamy, yogurt
2 garlic cloves, crushed
sea salt and freshly ground black
    pepper
2–3 tablespoons olive oil
1 red onion, cut in half lengthways,
    in half again crossways and sliced
    with the grain
1–2 teaspoons granulated sugar
1–2 teaspoons finely chopped dried
    red chilli/chile
2 tablespoons tiny currants, soaked
    in boiling water for 15 minutes
    and drained
2 tablespoons pine nuts
freshly squeezed juice of 1 lemon
warm crusty bread, to serve

Serves 3–4

Place the spinach in a steamer, or in a colander placed inside a large pot partially filled with water. Steam the spinach until soft. Drain off and squeeze out any excess water, then coarsely chop the steamed spinach.

In a bowl, beat the yogurt with the garlic. Season with salt and pepper and put aside.

Heat the oil in a heavy based pan and stir in the onion with the sugar for 2–3 minutes to soften. Add the chilli/chile, currants and pine nuts for 2–3 minutes, until the currants plump up and the pine nuts begin to colour. Toss in the spinach, making sure it is mixed well, and add the lemon juice. Season well with salt and pepper and tip the spinach onto a serving dish.

Make a well in the middle of the spinach and spoon some of the yogurt into it. Serve while the spinach is still warm with chunks of crusty bread to scoop it up.

Smoked aubergine with peppers, currants, yogurt and tahini

Arabian in origin, this is a delicious dish of smoked aubergine/eggplant and (bell) peppers with a lemony tang. There are numerous mezze dishes prepared with the flesh of smoked and baked aubergines/eggplants, such as 'baba ghanoush' (see page 38), but most of them are served cold. However, this dish, called 'ajvar', is delicious served warm, drizzled with cool yogurt and tahini.

2 aubergines/eggplants
2 red (bell) peppers
250 ml/1 cup thick, creamy yogurt
2 garlic cloves, crushed
sea salt and freshly ground
    black pepper
2–3 tablespoons olive oil
1 red onion, cut in half lengthways,
    and sliced along the grain
1 teaspoon finely chopped dried
    red chilli/chile, or 1 fresh red
    chilli/chile, with stalk and seeds
    removed, and finely sliced
2 tablespoons tiny currants, soaked
    in boiling water for 15 minutes
    and drained
1–2 teaspoons granulated sugar
freshly squeezed juice of 1 lemon
a dash of white wine vinegar
a bunch of fresh flat-leaf parsley,
    finely chopped
a small bunch of fresh mint leaves,
    finely chopped
1–2 tablespoons light tahini
warm crusty bread, to serve

Serves 3–4

Place the aubergines/eggplants and (bell) peppers directly over the gas flame, or over a charcoal grill. Once the skin has buckled and charred, place them in a resealable plastic bag to sweat. One at a time, hold them under cold running water and peel off the skins. Squeeze out the excess water.

Place the aubergines/eggplants on a board, chop off the stalk and chop the flesh to a coarse pulp. Place the (bell) peppers onto a board, cut them in half, remove the stalks and seeds, and chop the flesh to a pulp.

Beat the yogurt in a bowl with the garlic and season well with salt and pepper. Put aside.

Tip the olive oil into a wide, heavy-based pan and toss in the onion, chilli/chile, and sugar, until they begin to colour. Add the currants and let them plump up before tossing in the pulped pepper and aubergine/eggplant. Stir in the lemon juice and vinegar, season well with salt and pepper, and toss in most of the parsley and mint.

Spoon the hot aubergine/eggplant and pepper mixture onto a serving dish. Drizzle the tahini over the yogurt mixture. If you like, you can make a well in the middle of the aubergine/eggplant mixture and spoon the yogurt into it. Scatter the rest of the parsley and mint over the top. Serve immediately with chunks of fresh, crusty bread.

Garlicky potato purée with olive oil, lemon and parsley

This is one of those mezze dishes that some people insist on serving cold, others hot. Personally, for both the texture and the flavour, I prefer it hot, drizzled with olive oil, and served with lemon to squeeze over it. Even if you serve it cold, the mixture tastes better if you combine the ingredients when the potatoes are hot.

700 g/1½ lbs. potatoes (a fluffy variety suitable for mashing)
4 tablespoons olive oil
2–3 garlic cloves, crushed
freshly squeezed juice of 1 lemon
a small bunch of fresh dill, finely chopped
sea salt and freshly ground black pepper
2–3 spring onions/scallions, finely sliced
a small bunch of fresh flat-leaf parsley, finely chopped

Serves 4–6

Boil the potatoes in plenty of salted water until they are soft. Drain, peel off their skins, and put them into a bowl. Using a potato masher, pound the potatoes with most of the olive oil. Beat in the garlic, lemon juice and dill, and season well with salt and pepper.

Spoon the hot mashed potato onto a serving dish, drizzle with the rest of the oil, and scatter the spring onions/scallions and parsley over the top.

FRIED & SAUTÉED DISHES

Sautéed mushrooms with dukkah

Quick and easy, this is a great way to enjoy mushrooms. You can use any mushrooms you choose, although, because the flavour of the spice mix is quite strong, it might be a little overpowering for the subtle tastes of some wild mushrooms. For ease and availability, I often use chestnut mushrooms.

1–2 tablespoons Samna (see page 19) or 1–2 tablespoons olive oil with a knob/pat of butter
2–3 garlic cloves, finely chopped
600 g/1 lb. 5 oz. closed cup or chestnut mushrooms, rubbed clean and quartered

1–2 tablespoons Dukkah (see page 15)
1–2 teaspoons dried mint
sea salt and freshly ground black pepper
1 lemon, quartered

Serves 4

Heat the Samna (or olive oil and butter) in a wide, heavy-based pan and stir in the garlic for 1–2 minutes, until it begins to colour. Add the mushrooms, tossing them around the pan at intervals, until they have browned and shrunk in size. Toss in the Dukkah and dried mint and season well with salt and pepper – if you've made your own dukkah spice you'll know if it's salty and contains mint, so adjust the flavour accordingly. Tip the mushrooms into a bowl and serve with lemon to squeeze over them.

Ladies' fingers with lemon

Okra or ladies' fingers are particularly popular in Egypt and Oman but are often overcooked in stews, causing them to go soft and slimy. In this mezze dish, though, the okra are literally flicked around the pan so they stay crunchy. To ensure that the ladies' fingers or okra retain their green colour, they are soaked in lemon juice first.

300 g/10 oz. okra, rinsed, patted dry, and left whole
freshly squeezed juice of 2 lemons
2 tablespoons olive oil
1–2 teaspoons granulated sugar
sea salt and freshly ground black pepper

Serves 4

Put the okra into a wide bowl and toss them in the lemon juice. Leave them to soak for 10 minutes. Drain the okra through a colander but reserve the lemon juice.

Heat the oil in a wide, heavy-based pan, or in a curved pan like a wok, and toss in the okra for 2 minutes. Sprinkle the sugar over them and keep tossing for 1–2 minutes. Pour in the reserved lemon juice and keep tossing, until the okra are tender but still retain a bite.

Season the okra with salt and pepper and transfer them to a serving dish. Bubble up any liquid left in the pan to slightly caramelize it and drizzle it over the okra. Eat with your fingers while still hot.

Turmeric potatoes with lemon, chillies and coriander

With all its beneficial properties, turmeric is a wonderful ingredient in both its fresh and dried form. It plays a principal role in my version of the classic potato dish, 'battata harra'. With a liberal portion of ground turmeric, a fiery kick from the chillies/chiles and a refreshing burst of lemon, this adaptation has caught the eye of several chefs on my workshops.

700 g/1½ lbs. new potatoes
2 tablespoons Samna (see page 19) or 2 tablespoons olive oil with a knob/pat of butter
2–3 garlic cloves, finely chopped
1–2 teaspoons finely chopped dried red chilli/chile, or 1 fresh red chilli/chile, deseeded and finely chopped
1–2 teaspoons cumin seeds
2 teaspoons coriander seeds
1 tablespoon ground turmeric
freshly squeezed juice of 2 lemons
sea salt and freshly ground black pepper
a bunch of fresh coriander/cilantro, finely chopped (reserve a little for garnishing)
1 lime, cut into wedges

Serves 4-6

Place the potatoes in a steamer with their skins on and steam for about 10–15 minutes, until cooked but still firm. Drain and refresh under running cold water and carefully peel off the skins. Place the potatoes on a wooden board and cut them into bite-sized chunks.

Heat the Samna (or olive oil and butter) in a heavy-based pan and stir in the garlic, chilli/chile, cumin and coriander seeds for 2–3 minutes, then toss in the potatoes, coating them in the spices. Add the turmeric, making sure it coats the potatoes and pour in the lemon juice. Cook the potatoes in the turmeric and lemon juice for 2–3 minutes so they take on the colour and flavour.

Season the potatoes well with salt and pepper and toss in most of the coriander/cilantro. Tip the potatoes onto a serving dish, garnish with the rest of the coriander/cilantro and serve hot with the wedges of lime to squeeze over them.

Golden hallumi with zahtar

In Lebanon, Syria, Turkey, and both sides of Cyprus, hallumi is enjoyed in a number ways – grilled or fried, added to rice and salads, or as a filling for sweet and savoury pastries. Made from cow's milk and matured in whey, and sometimes combined with nigella seeds, mint, thyme or black olives, it is rubbery in texture but softens on cooking. Bland to taste on its own, it marries very well with spices and condiments. As a perfect nibble to go with a drink, I often fry it in olive oil and toss it in zahtar.

3–4 tablespoons olive oil
250 g/9 oz. plain hallumi, well rinsed, and cut into thin, bite-sized slices
1–2 tablespoons Zahtar (see page 12)
sea salt

Serves 3-4

Heat the oil in a heavy-based frying pan/skillet. Toss in the hallumi and fry for 4–5 minutes until golden brown all over. Drain on paper towels.

Tip the hot hallumi onto a serving dish and toss in the Zahtar. Sprinkle a little sea salt over the top and serve immediately, as you must eat it while it is still warm!

Spicy bean balls

Everyone is familiar with falafel, the spicy bean balls of Egypt, Jordan, Israel and the Palestinian territories, where they are often regarded as the national dish. Prepared with dried chickpeas or dried broad/fava beans, or a combination of the two, falafel can be tucked into the hollow pocket of toasted pitta bread with a sprinkling of sliced red onion, coarsely chopped parsley and a dollop of yogurt; they can also be served with pickles and a smidgeon of Harissa (see page 12) or Zhug (see page 16), or with garlic-flavoured yogurt and a drizzle of tahini.

350 g/12 oz. large, skinless, dried broad/fava beans, soaked for 24 hours
6 garlic cloves, crushed
1–2 teaspoons salt
2 teaspoons ground cumin
2 teaspoons ground coriander
1 scant teaspoon chilli powder or cayenne pepper
1 teaspoon baking powder
a bunch of fresh flat-leaf parsley, finely chopped (reserve a little for garnishing)
a bunch of fresh coriander/cilantro, finely chopped (reserve a little for garnishing)
4 spring onions/scallions, trimmed and finely chopped
sunflower oil, for frying
lemon wedges

Serves 4–6

Drain the broad/fava beans, put them into a food processor, and blend to a smooth soft paste – be advised, however, that this can take quite a long time. Add 4 of the crushed garlic cloves, salt, cumin, coriander, chilli powder and baking powder and continue to blend the paste. Add the herbs and spring onions/scallions and whizz briefly. Leave the mixture to rest for 1–2 hours for the flavours to mingle.

Mould the mixture into small, tight balls and place them on a plate. Heat up enough oil for deep-frying in a heavy-based pan, or a curved pan like a wok, and fry the broad/fava bean balls in batches, until golden brown. Drain them on paper towels.

Tip the falafel onto a serving dish and sprinkle the reserved parsley and coriander/cilantro over them. Serve with wedges of lemon to squeeze over them or with any of the suggestions above.

FROM LEFT TO RIGHT: Spicy bean balls;
Turmeric potatoes with lemon, chillies and
coriander; Golden hallumi with zahtar.

Courgette, feta and herb patties

These fried patties should be packed with herbs – the more the merrier – especially the mint. The patties are versatile, so you can also use grated raw carrot or fried leeks if you choose. Once cooked, they keep well and can be enjoyed cold as well as hot, straight out of the pan.

3 eggs

3 tablespoons plain/all-purpose flour

2 firm courgettes/zucchini

1 red or gold onion, cut in half
    lengthways, in half again
    crossways, and sliced with the grain

200 g/7 oz. feta, crumbled

1–2 fresh red or green chillies/chiles,
    deseeded and finely chopped

2 teaspoons dried mint

a bunch of fresh flat-leaf parsley,
    coarsely chopped

bunch of dill fronds, coarsely chopped

a big bunch of fresh mint leaves,
    coarsely chopped (reserve a little
    finely chopped mint for
    garnishing)

sea salt and freshly ground
    black pepper

sunflower oil, for frying

1–2 lemons, cut into wedges

Serves 6

In a big bowl, beat the eggs with the flour until smooth.

Trim off the ends of the courgettes/zucchini, but don't peel them. Grate the courgette/zucchini on the widest teeth of the grater, then squeeze out all of the water with your hands, then pile the courgette/zucchini all on top of the flour and egg mixture.

Add the onion, feta, chillies/chiles, dried mint and fresh herbs and mix well with a large spoon or your hand. Season the mixture well with salt and pepper.

Heat a little sunflower oil in a heavy-based frying pan/skillet – don't put in too much oil; you can always add more as you fry the patties. Place 2–3 spoonfuls of the courgette/zucchini mixture into the pan and fry over a medium heat for about 2 minutes each side, pressing the patties down a little with the spatula, so that they are flat but quite thick, lightly browned and firm. Cook the patties in batches, adding more oil to the pan when necessary, drain on paper towels, and keep the cooked ones warm under aluminium foil, or in a warm oven.

Arrange the patties on a serving dish, garnish with the reserved mint, and serve with wedges of lemon to squeeze over them.

Crispy vegetables fried in turmeric yeast batter with ketchup dip

Deep-fried vegetables served with a fiery or creamy dip are popular on a mezze table. You can use any vegetables of your choice, including thin slices of pumpkin, butternut squash, broccoli, (bell) peppers, and whole chillies/chiles. Simply adjust the quantities accordingly and serve with Tahini and Lemon Dip with Parsley (see page 34), Roasted Red Pepper and Walnut Dip (see page 37), or a fiery dip prepared with Harissa (see page 12) or Zhug (see page 16) combined with enough oil to make it suitable for dipping. If you have children, a family favourite accompaniment for deep-fried vegetables, shellfish and falafel is garlic-flavoured yogurt combined with tomato ketchup, which I felt I should include here!

2 carrots, peeled, halved and cut
  into long slices
2 courgettes/zucchini, halved and
  cut into long strips
6–8 cauliflower florets
3–4 spring onions/scallions,
  trimmed and halved
sunflower oil, for deep frying

For the batter:
1 teaspoon dried yeast granules
1 scant teaspoon caster/granulated
  sugar
175 g/1¼ cups plus 1 tablespoon
  chickpea/gram flour
1 tablespoon ground turmeric
salt
2 tablespoons thick, creamy yogurt

For the dip:
6 heaped tablespoons thick,
  creamy yogurt
2 garlic cloves, crushed
sea salt and freshly ground
  black pepper
1–2 tablespoons tomato ketchup

Serves 4–6

First, prepare the batter. In a small bowl, combine the yeast and sugar with 50 ml/3 tablespoons warm water and leave it to froth. Sift the flour and turmeric with a pinch of salt into a bowl, make a well in the middle, and tip in the creamed yeast with the yogurt and 200 ml/¾ cup plus 1 tablespoon warm water. Using a balloon whisk, combine the mixture to form a smooth batter, and leave it to stand for 30 minutes.

Meanwhile, prepare the dip. In a small bowl, beat together the yogurt and garlic and season with salt and pepper. Beat in the ketchup.

Heat enough sunflower oil for deep frying in a heavy-based pan, or in a curved pan like a wok. Dip the sliced vegetables and florets into the batter, one at a time, and slip them into the hot oil. Fry them in batches until crisp and golden brown – some will take longer than others – and drain them on paper towels.

Tip the crispy fried vegetables onto a serving dish and enjoy dipping them into the ketchup dip!

PASTRIES & PIES

Little spinach and feta pastries with pine nuts

These little pastries ('fatayer') can be stuffed with ingredients like spinach, pumpkin, dry-cured beef, shellfish and cheese, and they are usually shaped into triangles and squares.

500 g/1 lb. 2 oz. fresh spinach leaves,
   trimmed, washed and drained
2 tablespoons olive oil, plus extra
   for brushing
1 tablespoon butter
2 onions, chopped
3 heaped tablespoons pine nuts
   (reserve 1 tablespoon for
   garnishing)
freshly squeezed juice of 1 lemon
1 teaspoon ground allspice
150 g/5¼ oz. feta, crumbled with
   your fingers
a small bunch of fresh dill,
   finely chopped
sea salt and freshly ground
   black pepper
plain/all-purpose flour, for dusting
450 g/16 oz. ready-prepared
   puff pastry

Serves 6

Preheat the oven to 180°C (360°F) Gas 4.

Steam the spinach until soft and floppy, then drain and refresh under running cold water and squeeze out the excess liquid with your hands. Place the spinach on a wooden board and chop it coarsely.

Heat the oil and butter in a heavy-based pan and stir in the onion to soften. Add the pine nuts and cook for 2–3 minutes until both the onions and pine nuts begin to turn golden. Stir in the spinach with the lemon juice and allspice and lightly toss in the crumbled feta and dill. Season the mixture with a little salt and pepper and leave to cool.

Lightly dust a surface with flour and roll the pastry into a thin sheet. Using a pastry cutter, or the rim of a cup, cut out as many 10-cm/4-in. rounds as you can and pile them up, lightly dusting them with flour. Take each round and spoon a little of the spinach mixture in the middle. Pull up the sides to make a pyramid by pinching the edges with your fingertips – it does not matter if one of the sides opens during cooking to reveal the filling, as that is part of their appeal.

Lightly grease two baking sheets and place the pastries on them. Brush the tops with a little oil and bake them in the preheated oven for about 30 minutes, until golden brown.

Roughly 5 minutes before taking the pastries out of the oven, spread the reserved tablespoon of pine nuts onto a small piece of aluminium foil and toast them in the oven until they turn golden brown. Once you have placed the little pastries on a plate, sprinkle the toasted pine nuts over them and serve while they are still hot.

TOP RIGHT: Little spinach and feta pastries with pine nuts
RIGHT: Filo cigars filled with feta, parsley, mint and dill (see page 86)

Filo cigars filled with feta, parsley, mint and dill

Almost every restaurant and household prepares these classic cigar-shaped pastries on a regular basis, and they are devoured in quantity. Moroccans often add finely chopped preserved lemon to the filling and the Greeks tend to use mint on its own for flavouring and to drizzle the fried cigars with honey. The cigars can be prepared in advance and kept under a clean, damp tea/dish towel in the refrigerator until you are ready to deep-fry them at the last minute.

225 g/8 oz. feta

1 large egg, lightly beaten

*a small bunch of fresh flat-leaf
     parsley, finely chopped*

*a small bunch of fresh dill,
     finely chopped*

*a small bunch of fresh mint,
     finely chopped*

4–5 sheets of filo/phyllo pastry

sunflower oil, for deep frying

dill fronds for garnishing (optional)

Serves 4

In a bowl, mash the feta with a fork. Beat in the egg and fold in the herbs.

Place the sheets of filo/phyllo under a damp tea/dish towel to keep them moist and work with one at a time. Cut the sheets into strips, roughly 10–13 cm/4–5 in. wide, and pile them on top of each other. Lay one strip on the surface in front of you. Place a heaped teaspoon of the cheese filling along one end. Roll the end of the filo/phyllo over the filling, quite tightly to keep it in place, then tuck in the edges to seal in the filling, and continue to roll the filo/phyllo into a cigar until you get to the other end. Just as you reach the end, brush the tip with a little water to help seal the filo/phyllo, so it doesn't unravel on cooking. Place the filled cigar on a plate under a damp tea/dish towel to keep it moist and continue with the remaining sheets of filo/phyllo.

In a deep-sided pan/skillet, heat enough oil for deep frying. Fry the filo/phyllo cigars in batches until crisp and golden brown. Lift them out of the oil and drain on paper towels. Serve immediately, garnished with dill fronds, if you like.

Pastry triangles filled with tuna and egg

If you are serving these pastries ('brik') as finger-food, there is an art to eating them, as the egg is designed to be runny. Hold the pastry by the corner and take a big bite into the middle to catch the yolk before it dribbles down your chin. These make great mezze snacks at any time of the day.

1 tablespoon olive oil

1 onion, finely chopped

6–8 anchovy fillets

1 x 200-g/7-oz. can of tuna, rinsed and drained

1 tablespoon capers, rinsed and drained

a small bunch of fresh flat-leaf parsley, finely chopped

2 sheets filo/phyllo pastry, cut into 4 x 20-cm/8-inch squares

4 eggs

Serves 4

Heat the oil in a frying pan/skillet and stir in the onion for 2 minutes to soften it. Add the anchovies and fry until they melt into the oil. Turn off the heat and leave the mixture to cool.

Tip the onion mixture into a bowl and add the tuna. Break up the tuna with a fork and add the capers and parsley. Mix well.

Place the filo/phyllo squares on a work surface and spoon a quarter of the mixture onto one half of each square in the shape of a triangle. You can prepare one at a time and fry it immediately, or you can prepare all of them at once, but you have to work quickly. Make a well in the tuna mixture and crack an egg into it. Fold the empty side of the filo/phyllo over the filling, taking care not to move or burst the egg, and seal the edges with a little water.

Heat enough oil for frying in a heavy-based frying pan/skillet and slip one of the pastries into the oil. Fry 1–2 at a time, depending on the size of your pan/skillet, for less than 1 minute each side. When crisp and golden brown, lift the pastry out of the pan and drain it on paper towels. Repeat with the other pastries and serve warm while the yolk is still runny.

Baked shellfish and coriander pastry

These pastries ('rghaif') can be baked in the oven or cooked on a griddle. Instead of shellfish, other traditional fillings include sautéed strips of chicken flavoured with saffron, or roasted vegetables and cheese.

sunflower oil, for working
   the dough
1 egg yolk mixed with
   1 tablespoon water, for
   brushing

For the dough:
15 g/1 tablespoon fresh yeast
   or 1½ teaspoons
   dried/active dry yeast
400 ml/1½ cups plus
   3 tablespoons warm water
350 g/2½ cups plus
   1 tablespoon plain/
   all-purpose flour
1 teaspoon salt
175 ml/¾ cup sunflower oil

For the filling:
2–3 tablespoons olive oil and
   a knob of butter
2 onions, finely chopped
2 garlic cloves, crushed
1 red or green chilli/chile,
   deseeded and finely chopped

1 teaspoon ground cumin
1 teaspoon ground coriander
1 teaspoon paprika, plus a
   little extra for dusting
175 g/6¼ oz. small fresh
   prawns/shrimp, shelled
   and deveined
175 g/6¼ oz. small squid,
   with ink sack, back bone
   and head removed, and
   thinly sliced
a bunch of fresh coriander/
   cilantro, finely chopped
a small bunch of fresh
   flat-leaf parsley,
   finely chopped
freshly squeezed juice of
   1 lemon
sea salt and freshly ground
   black pepper

Serves 4–6

In a small bowl, cream the yeast with roughly 100 ml/7 tablespoons of the warm water and leave it in a warm place to froth.

Sift the flour with the salt into a wide bowl and make a well in the centre. Pour the oil and the yeast into the well. Gradually add the rest of the water as you draw the flour in from the sides and knead the mixture with your hands to form a smooth, soft dough.

Divide the dough into 12 balls and place them on a lightly oiled work surface under a damp tea/dish towel. Leave to prove for about 1 hour, until they have doubled in size.

Meanwhile, prepare the filling. Heat the olive oil with the butter in a heavy-based pan and stir in the onions, garlic and chilli/chile for 2–3 minutes, until they begin to colour. Stir in the spices and toss in the prawns/shrimp and squid. Add the herbs and lemon juice and season with salt and pepper. Turn off the heat and leave the mixture to cool.

Preheat the oven to 180°C (360°F) Gas 4.

On an oiled work surface, spread and stretch each dough ball with your fingers to form a thin circle. Put a large spoonful of the mixture just off-centre in each circle. Fold the narrower edge over the mixture, tuck in the ends, then fold the wider edge over to seal in the mixture and form a square package.

Place the pastries sealed-side down on an oiled baking sheet and brush each one with a little of the egg-yolk mixture. Bake the pastries in the preheated oven for about 30 minutes, until crisp and golden. Dust them with a little paprika and eat immediately.

TOP RIGHT: Baked shellfish and coriander pastry
RIGHT: Pastry triangles filled with tuna and egg
(see page 87)

Vine leaf pie with yogurt and herbs

Vine leaves are not only stuffed with savoury rice and rolled into little fat logs they are also pickled, wrapped around fish, chicken, or cheese and grilled, and they form the casing of this wonderful pie. If you pick or buy fresh vine leaves, they need to be softened in a bowl of boiling water for less than a minute and refreshed in cold water. Preserved leaves, on the other hand, need to be soaked in several changes of cold water for at least 1 hour to remove the salt (see page 59).

3–4 tablespoons olive oil

a knob/pat of butter

4 spring onions/scallions, finely sliced

12–16 fresh or preserved vine leaves, washed and prepared as above

4–6 tablespoons thick, creamy yogurt

a small bunch of fresh flat-leaf parsley, finely chopped

a small bunch of fresh dill, finely chopped

a small bunch of fresh mint, finely chopped

4 tablespoons rice flour

sea salt and freshly ground black pepper

2 tablespoons sesame seeds

Serves 4–6

Preheat the oven to 180°C (360°F) Gas 4.

Heat 1 tablespoon of the olive oil in a frying pan/skillet and toss in the spring onions/scallions until they begin to brown. Turn off the heat and leave to cool.

Heat the rest of the olive oil with the butter in a small pot until the butter has melted. Brush a little of the mixture over the base and sides of a shallow ovenproof dish. Line the base of the dish with half of the vine leaves, brushing each one with the oil and letting them hang over the edge of the dish.

In a bowl, mix the yogurt with the herbs and browned spring onions/scallions. Season well with salt and pepper and beat in the rice flour. Tip the mixture into the middle of the leaves and spread it out evenly. Place the rest of the leaves on top, brushing each one with oil, and pull up the dangling sides to create a tight parcel.

Brush the rest of the oil over the top, sprinkle with the sesame seeds, and place the pie in the preheated oven for 45 minutes, until it is firm to the touch and the top leaves are crisp. Cut it into portions and serve hot.

STUFFED VEGETABLES & FRUIT

Roasted baby peppers stuffed with feta

Stuffed peppers are perhaps the best known of the stuffed vegetables prepared for mezze. The most traditional are the small green ones stuffed with aromatic rice and served cold, or the larger (bell) peppers stuffed with minced/ground lamb and served hot, but I like to roast the brightly coloured baby peppers and stuff them with feta. I often combine them with thin strips of saffron pear (see page 124), or I drizzle a little honey over them to enhance the sweet and salty balance.

500 g/1 lb. 2 oz. baby red, yellow and
    orange (bell) peppers
2–3 tablespoons olive oil
300 g/10½ oz. feta, rinsed and
    drained
1–2 teaspoons finely chopped dried
    red chilli, or paprika
2–3 teaspoons dried oregano
1 tablespoon runny honey
1–2 tablespoons pine nuts
a bunch of fresh basil leaves

Serves 4–6

Preheat the oven to 200°C (400°F) Gas 6.

Using a small sharp knife, cut the stalks off the (bell) peppers and take out the seeds. Rinse and drain the peppers and place them in a baking dish. Pour over 2 tablespoons of the oil and place them in the preheated oven for about 45 minutes, turning them over from time to time until they have softened and are beginning to buckle.

Meanwhile, crumble the feta into a bowl and fold in the rest of the olive oil with the chilli and oregano.

Take the (bell) peppers out of the oven and let them cool a little, until you can handle them. Using your fingers, carefully stuff the feta mixture into each pepper. Be careful not to overstuff them as the skin will split. Lightly squeeze the tips of the peppers together to prevent the feta from spilling out and pop them back into the preheated oven for 15 minutes.

Drizzle the honey over them and return them to the oven for 5–10 minutes. Tip the pine nuts into a small pan and dry-roast them for 1–2 minutes, until golden brown. Sprinkle the roasted pine nuts on top and serve.

Baked aubergine boats with mint yogurt

This is a traditional village method of cooking aubergines/eggplants. When the communal oven was fired up for bread, villagers would often put in vegetables, a piece of meat, or a stew to profit from the heat. Although many villagers now have simple gas or electric ovens, the tradition still carries on in some regions, and I have enjoyed these hot, freshly baked aubergines/eggplants with a garlicky tomato sauce and with melted goat's cheese, but my favourite way is with cool, creamy garlic-flavoured yogurt spiked with fresh mint and eaten with a spoon like a melon.

6 baby or 2 long, slim
aubergines/eggplants
1–2 tablespoons olive oil
sea salt and freshly ground
black pepper
500 ml/2 cups thick,
creamy yogurt
2 garlic cloves, crushed
a bunch of fresh mint leaves,
finely chopped (reserve some
for garnishing)
2 tablespoons fresh pomegranate
seeds

Serves 4

Preheat the oven to 200°C (400°F) Gas 6.

Cut the aubergines/eggplants in half, lengthways, right through the stalks and place them on a lightly oiled baking dish or sheet. Brush the tops with some olive oil, sprinkle with salt and pepper, and place them in the preheated oven for 25 minutes.

Using your fingers, lightly press down the middles of the aubergines/eggplants if the flesh is soft enough, brush with oil again, and return them to the oven for 15 minutes, until the flesh is soft and nicely browned.

Meanwhile, beat the yogurt with the garlic in a bowl and season well with salt and pepper. Beat in most of the mint.

Take the aubergines/eggplants out of the oven and arrange them on a serving dish. Using a sharp knife, make two or three criss-cross incisions into the flesh and press down the middle to form a hollow for the yogurt. Spoon the yogurt into each one and garnish with the reserved mint and pomegranate seeds.

Serve immediately, while the aubergines/eggplants are still hot, and eat them with a spoon, scooping out the flesh with the yogurt, leaving the skin behind.

Roasted meat-stuffed onions with tamarind and butter

Variations of this traditional recipe, 'makshi basal', crop up all over Iran, Turkey, Syria, Jordan, Israel and the Palestinian territories, where it can be served as a hot mezze dish, or as a main course. Large golden or red onions are ideal for this dish, as the layers can be easily unravelled, stuffed and rolled up again.

2–3 large onions, peeled and left whole

250 g/9 oz. lean minced/ground lamb

90 g/½ cup long-grain rice, rinsed and drained

1 tablespoon tomato purée/paste

2 teaspoons ground cinnamon

1 teaspoon ground allspice

1 teaspoon ground cumin

1 teaspoon ground coriander

a small bunch of fresh flat-leaf parsley, finely chopped (reserve a little for garnishing)

sea salt and freshly ground black pepper

2 tablespoons olive oil

1 tablespoon tamarind paste

2 teaspoons runny honey

1 tablespoon butter

1 lemon, cut into wedges

Serves 4–6

Preheat the oven to 200°C (400°F) Gas 6.

Bring a pot of water to the boil. Cut each onion down one side from the top to the bottom and pop them into the boiling water for about 10 minutes, until they are soft and begin to unravel. Drain and refresh the onions and separate the layers.

In a bowl, pound the meat, slapping it down into the bowl. Add the rice, tomato purée/paste, spices, parsley and seasoning and knead well, making sure it is thoroughly mixed.

Spread the onion layers out on a clean surface and place a spoonful of the meat mixture into each one. Roll them up loosely, leaving room for the rice to expand on cooking. Tuck in the ends and pack the stuffed onions close together in a heavy-based pot or ovenproof dish. Mix together the olive oil, tamarind paste and honey with roughly 125 ml/½ cup water and pour it over the stuffed onions.

Cover the pot or dish with a lid or aluminium foil and pop it in the preheated oven for about 25 minutes, until the rice has expanded.

Melt the butter in small pot and pour it over the stuffed onions. Place them back in the oven, uncovered for 15–20 minutes, until nicely browned on top and slightly caramelized.

Arrange the stuffed onions on a serving dish and drizzle any leftover tamarind butter over them. Garnish with the reserved parsley and serve them hot with wedges of lemon to squeeze over them.

Baby aubergines stuffed with minced lamb, ras el hanout and dried rose petals

Often referred to as 'poor man's meat', as they're much cheaper than meat and because they grow in abundance in the Middle East, aubergines/eggplants are cooked in infinite ways. This is one of my mezze versions of the Ottoman classic, 'karnıyarık', in which I've combined flavours from east and west. If you can't find baby aubergines/eggplants, you can adapt the recipe for 2–3 medium-sized ones and then cut them into 2–3 pieces when serving.

6 baby aubergines/eggplants
sunflower oil, for frying
150 ml/½ cup plus 2 tablespoons
    olive oil
50 ml/3 tablespoons water
1–2 tablespoons runny honey
1–2 tablespoons pine nuts
1 tablespoon dried rose petals
1 lemon, cut into wedges

For the filling:
1 tablespoon olive oil
I onion, finely chopped
2 garlic cloves, finely chopped
175 g/6 oz. finely minced/ground
    lean lamb
2 teaspoons ground cinnamon
1–2 teaspoons ras el hanout
    spice mix
1 tablespoon pine nuts
a small bunch of fresh flat-leaf
    parsley, finely chopped
sea salt and freshly ground
    black pepper

Serves 6

Preheat the oven to 200°C (400°F) Gas 6.

First prepare the filling. Heat the olive oil in a small pan and stir in the onion and garlic for 1–2 minutes, until they begin to colour. Turn off the heat and leave to cool.

Put the minced/ground lamb into a bowl and add the softened onion and garlic, cinnamon, ras el hanout, pine nuts and parsley. Season well, as all the flavour for this dish comes from the filling. Using your hands, knead the mixture for a few minutes, until thoroughly combined. Put aside.

Using a sharp knife or a potato peeler, partially peel the aubergines in thick stripes, like the markings of a zebra. Immerse the whole aubergines/eggplants in a bowl of salted water for 15 minutes, then drain and pat dry. Heat enough sunflower oil for frying in a heavy-based frying pan and pop in the aubergines/eggplants, rolling them in the oil until they are lightly browned all over. Lift them out of the oil and drain on paper towels.

Using a knife or tongs, slit each aubergine/eggplant lengthways down the middle, taking care not to cut through the base and making sure you leave the ends intact, so that it resembles a kayak. Prise each slit open and divide the meat mixture amongst them, making sure the filling is tightly packed.

Place the stuffed aubergines/eggplants, side by side, in a baking dish. Mix together the olive oil and water and pour it over and around the aubergines/eggplants. Sprinkle a little salt over the top, cover the dish with aluminium foil, and pop it in the preheated oven for about 30 minutes.

Remove the foil, drizzle the honey over the aubergines/eggplants, and scatter the pine nuts on top. Return the dish, uncovered, to the oven for 5 minutes, until the pine nuts are golden brown.

Arrange the aubergines/eggplants on a serving dish, drizzle some of the sweet cooking juices over them, and garnish with the dried rose petals. Serve hot with wedges of lemon to squeeze over them.

Roasted butternut sickle moons with dukkah and lime

Combinations of garlic and spices always work well with the mild, but slightly perfumed, flesh of butternut squash. When you add these to the mezze table, you can eat them with your fingers or run a knife between the flesh and the skin to separate them.

1 medium butternut squash, weighing approximately 900 g/2 lbs.
2–3 tablespoons olive oil
1 tablespoon Dukkah (see page 15)
sea salt
1 teaspoon dried mint
2 limes, quartered

Serves 4–6

Cut the butternut squash in half lengthways, scoop out the seeds, and cut each half crossways into thin slices. The slices in middle with the hollow will look like sickle moons, whereas the others will resemble half moons.

Lightly grease a baking dish or sheet, and place the butternut slices on it. In a small bowl, mix the Dukkah with the olive oil and brush the mixture over the slices. Sprinkle with salt and pop them into the preheated oven for about 15 minutes.

Baste the slices with any of the spicy oil in the dish, sprinkle with the dried mint, and tuck the lime wedges in and around them. Return them to the oven for another 10 minutes, or until they are tender. Arrange the butternut sickle moons on a serving dish, drizzle with any spicy oil in the baking dish, and serve with the hot lime wedges to squeeze over them.

Roasted aubergines with dates, harissa and fennel seeds

This is a vegan dish that I devised with a group of Middle Eastern chefs who wanted to come up with new ideas for vegetarians and vegans – something alien to most inhabitants in that part of the world, where there is deeply ingrained love of all things dairy.

2 aubergines/eggplants, cut into bite-sized chunks
sea salt
1 teaspoon coriander seeds
2 teaspoons roasted fennel seeds
2–3 tablespoons olive oil
8 moist, dried dates, cut into 4 lengthways
1 x 400-g/14-oz. can of tomatoes, drained of juice
1–2 teaspoons Harissa (see page 12)
1–2 teaspoons granulated sugar
a bunch of fresh coriander/cilantro, finely chopped

Serves 4–6

Preheat the oven to 200°C (400°F) Gas 6.

Sprinkle the aubergines/eggplants with salt and leave them to weep for 5–10 minutes. Rinse them in cold water and pat dry.

Spread out the aubergine/eggplant chunks in an ovenproof dish, scatter the coriander and fennel seeds over them, and add a good glug of olive oil. Pop them into the preheated oven for 20 minutes, then toss in the dates and return the dish to the oven for about 10 minutes.

In a bowl combine the drained tomatoes with the Harissa and sugar. Add the mixture to the aubergines/eggplants and dates, making sure they are coated in it, and return the dish to the oven for 15–20 minutes.

Toss in most of the coriander/cilantro and spoon the mixture into a serving bowl. Garnish with the rest of the coriander/cilantro and serve while hot.

Baked dates stuffed with harissa couscous

The Bedouin dream of dates, as they are so sweet and satisfying, but they dangle from high palms out of the reach of these desert nomads. Since ancient times, they have provided enough nutrition for a man to journey across the desert on a diet solely of dates. They have been enjoyed in both their fresh and dried forms, pounded to a paste, and simmered into syrup, so it is no wonder that they have found their way into many sweet and savoury recipes like this mezze dish, which is Moroccan in character.

110 g/⅔ cup couscous
½ teaspoon salt
150 ml/½ cup plus 2 tablespoons warm water
2 tablespoons olive oil
1 teaspoon Harissa (see page 12)
1 teaspoon runny honey
4–6 ready-to-eat dried apricots, finely chopped
a small bunch of fresh coriander/cilantro, finely chopped
12 large, ready-to-eat Medjool dates
freshly squeezed juice of 1 lemon or 1 small orange
25 g/2 tablespoons butter
2 tablespoons whole blanched almonds

Serves 4–6

Preheat the oven to 180°C (360°F) Gas 4.

Tip the couscous into a bowl. Stir the salt into the water and pour it over the couscous. Stir to make sure the water is absorbed evenly, then cover the bowl with a dampened tea/dish towel and leave the couscous to swell for about 10 minutes.

Rake the couscous with a fork to separate the grains and rub 1 tablespoon of the oil into them, aerating them with your fingertips. Rub in the Harissa and honey and toss in the chopped apricots and the coriander/cilantro.

Using a small sharp knife, slit the dates down one side to extract the stone and fill the cavity with the couscous, stuffing it in gently. Place the dates side by side in a baking dish and drizzle the remaining tablespoon of olive oil over them combined with the lemon or orange juice. Cover the dish with foil and place them in the preheated oven for 25 minutes to heat through.

Meanwhile, melt the butter in a pan and stir in the almonds, until they are golden brown. Lift the almonds out of the butter and separate into halves.

Arrange the stuffed dates on a serving dish and garnish each one with a halved, buttered almond. Drizzle a little of the almond butter over the top and serve while still warm.

KEBABS & PAN FRIES

Mini meatballs stuffed with roasted pistachios

Meatballs are prepared daily in the Middle Eastern region as mezze, street food, as main courses – there are so many types, I lose count. They are primarily prepared from minced/ground lamb or beef and, on occasion, minced/ground chicken or flaked fish. These mini ones, called 'cizbiz', are perfect mezze balls containing a bite of roasted pistachio in the middle and served with wedges of lemon to squeeze over them.

2–3 tablespoons pistachios, shelled

250 g/9 oz. lean minced/ground lamb

1 onion, finely chopped

2 garlic cloves, crushed

2 teaspoons ground cinnamon

a small bunch of fresh flat-leaf parsley, finely chopped

sea salt and freshly ground black pepper

sunflower oil

1–2 lemons, cut into wedges

Serves 4–6

In a small heavy-based pan, roast the pistachios for 1–2 minutes, until they emit a nutty aroma. Using a pestle and mortar, crush most of them lightly to break them into small pieces.

In a bowl, pound the minced/ground lamb with the onion, garlic and cinnamon. Knead it with your hands and slap the mixture down into the base of the bowl to knock out the air. Add the parsley and seasoning and knead well to make sure it is thoroughly mixed.

Take cherry-size portions of the mixture in your hands and roll them into balls. Indent each ball with your finger, right into the middle, and fill the hollow with a few of the crushed pistachios, and seal it by squeezing the mixture over it and then rolling the ball once more.

Heat a thin layer of oil in a heavy-based frying pan/skillet. Place the meatballs in the pan/skillet and cook them on all sides, until nicely browned. Drain on paper towels, sprinkle with the remaining crushed pistachios, and serve with lemon wedges to squeeze over them.

Mini kebabs with flatbreads, lemon and parsley

This is one of the few kebab/kabob dishes that can be included in mezze, as the pieces of meat are small and it is served in small portions. Wrapped in a freshly griddled flatbread with red onion, parsley and a squeeze of lemon, these kebabs/kabob are tender and tasty and well worth the effort of making them on a day that you are enjoying your mezze outdoors with a charcoal grill.

2 onions

½ tablespoon salt

2 garlic cloves, crushed

2 teaspoons cumin seeds, crushed

900 g/2 lbs. lean lamb, trimmed
    and cut into small bite-size pieces

For the flat bread:

225 g/1½ cups plus 1 tablespoon
    white strong/bread flour,
    plus extra for dusting

50 g/3 tablespoons
    wholemeal/wholewheat flour

1 teaspoon salt

200 ml/¾ cup plus 2 tablespoons
    lukewarm water

1–2 tablespoons Samna (see page 19)
    or 1–2 tablespoons olive oil with
    a knob/pat of butter

To serve:

1 large red onion, halved lengthways,
    cut in half again crossways, and
    sliced with the grain

a large bunch of fresh flat-leaf
    parsley, roughly chopped

2–3 lemons, halved

Serves 4-6

First, grate the onions onto a plate. Sprinkle the salt over the top and leave the onions to weep for about 15 minutes. Place a sieve/strainer over a bowl. Tip the weeping onion into the sieve/strainer, pressing it down with the back of a wooden spoon to extract the juice. Discard the onion that is left in the sieve/strainer. Mix the juice with the garlic and cumin seeds and toss in the lamb. Leave the lamb to marinade for 3–4 hours.

Meanwhile, prepare the dough for the flatbreads. Sift the flours with the salt into a bowl. Make a well in the centre and add the water gradually, drawing the flour in from the sides. Using your hands, knead the dough until firm and springy – if the dough is at all sticky, add more flour. Divide the dough into roughly 12 pieces and knead each one into a ball. Place the balls on a floured surface and cover with a damp cloth. Leave them to rest for about 30 minutes.

Prepare your charcoal grill. Just before cooking, roll out each ball of dough into wide, thin circles, keeping them dusted with flour so they don't stick together, and cover them with a clean, damp tea/dish towel to prevent them from drying out. Quickly thread the meat onto kebab/kabob swords, or metal skewers, and place them over the hot charcoal for 2–3 minutes each side.

At the same time, heat a flat pan or griddle at one end of the charcoal grill, or over a separate flame, and melt most of the Samna (or olive oil and butter) in a small pot. Brush the hot griddle or flat pan with a little of the remaining Samna (or olive oil and butter) and cook the flatbreads for about 15 seconds each side, flipping them over as soon as they begin to brown and buckle and continue brushing them with a little Samna (or olive oil and butter). Pile them up on plate and keep warm.

When the kebabs/kabobs are cooked, slide the meat off the skewers onto the flatbreads. Scatter some onion and parsley over each pile and squeeze the lemon juice over the top. Wrap the flatbread into parcels and eat with your hands.

Mother-in-law's meatballs

In the Anatolian region of Turkey, there is a traditional meatball dish prepared for a new bride by her mother-in-law. Great care is taken to pound bulgur with minced/ground beef or lamb to form balls, which are then hollowed out to create shells to contain the spicy filling before the sides are pushed together and sealed to form a ball again. The act of making and presenting these stuffed meatballs, 'içli köfte', is to signify that the lips of the new daughter-in-law must now be sealed with discretion. Variations of these meatballs are called 'kibbeh' in Syria, Lebanon and Jordan.

225 g /1¼ cups plus 1 tablespoon
  bulgur
225 g/8 oz. finely minced/ground
  beef or lamb
1–2 teaspoons very finely chopped
  dried red chilli/chile, or paprika
sea salt
plain/all-purpose flour, for coating
sunflower oil, for deep frying
a large bunch of fresh flat-leaf parsley

For the filling:
1–2 tablespoons Samna (see page 19)
  or 1–2 tablespoons olive oil with
  a knob/pat of butter
1 onion, finely chopped
4 garlic cloves, finely chopped
60 g/½ cup walnuts, finely chopped
60 g/½ cup pistachios,
  finely chopped
1 teaspoon ground cumin
1 teaspoon ground coriander
1 teaspoon dried thyme
120 g/4¼ oz. finely minced/ground
  beef or lamb
a small bunch of fresh flat-leaf
  parsley, finely chopped
sea salt and freshly ground
  black pepper

Serves 4–6

Melt the Samna (or olive oil and butter) in a heavy-based pan and stir in the onion and garlic until they begin to colour. Add the walnuts and pistachios and stir for 1–2 minutes, then toss in the spices, thyme and minced/ground meat and cook for 4–5 minutes, stirring occasionally. Stir in the parsley and season with salt and pepper. Leave the mixture to cool.

Meanwhile, put the bulgur into a bowl and pour in enough boiling water to just cover it. Cover the bowl and leave the bulgur to absorb the water for about 25 minutes. Squeeze the bulgur to make sure there is no excess water, then add the minced/ground meat, finely chopped chilli/chile, and season with salt. Using your hands, knead the ingredients together thoroughly.

Take a small portion of the mixture in the palm of your hand and mould it into a ball. Using a finger, hollow out an opening and put it on a flat surface. Repeat with the rest of the mixture.

Using a teaspoon, spoon a little filling into each hollow and pinch the edges together to seal. Gently squeeze the bulgur mixture together to form a ball, or a cone, and toss the balls in a little flour to lightly coat them.

Heat enough sunflower oil for deep-frying in a pan. Fry the meatballs in batches for 3–4 minutes, until golden brown. Drain on paper towels and serve hot on a bed of flat-leaf parsley to eat with them.

Ladies' thighs with sautéed pomegranate seeds

The Sultans of the Ottoman Empire were renowned for their lavish feasts and, during the reign of Suleyman the Magnificent, a number of sweet and savoury dishes acquired graphic names, such as 'sweethearts' lips', 'ladies' thighs' and 'girls' breasts'. Plump and juicy, these ladies' thighs, 'kadınbudu köfte', are replicated in other parts of the region as 'kibbeh'.

1 tablespoon olive oil

1 onion, finely chopped

500 g/1lb. 2 oz. lean minced/ground lamb or beef

120 g/1 cup cooked long- or medium-grain rice

a bunch of fresh flat-leaf parsley, finely chopped

1 teaspoon ground cumin

2 teaspoons ground cinnamon

1 teaspoon dried thyme

sea salt and freshly ground black pepper

plain/all-purpose flour for coating

2 eggs, beaten

sunflower oil, for frying

25 g/2 tablespoons butter

2 tablespoons fresh pomegranate seeds

Serves 4–6

Heat the olive oil in a heavy-based pan and stir in the onions, until they begin to colour. Add half of the minced/ground meat and fry over a high heat until all the liquid has evaporated. Add the cooked rice to the pan and mix well.

Tip the meat and rice mixture into a bowl. Add the rest of the raw minced/ground meat with the parsley and spices. Season well with salt and pepper and, using your hand, knead the mixture until it is thoroughly bound. Take apricot-sized portions of the mixture in the palm of your hand and mould them into oval shapes. Flatten them with the heel of your hand and dip them in the flour.

Heat enough oil for deep-frying in a pan. Dip the flour-coated 'thighs' into the beaten egg and drop them into the oil. Cook in batches for 2 minutes each side, until crisp and golden. Drain on paper towels and arrange on a serving dish.

Melt the butter in a small saucepan and stir in the pomegranate seeds for 1–2 minutes. Spoon them over the ladies' thighs and serve immediately.

Pan-fried lamb's liver with cumin and lemon

If you're not a liver enthusiast, this dish might change your mind. I often include it in my mezze workshops and I'm amazed at how many people do actually become converts. In restaurants, the liver is often cooked in olive oil and served as a cold mezze dish, but I prefer it cooked in samna and served hot with lots of lemon to squeeze over it – the lemon is crucial, as it lifts the texture and flavour of the liver.

500 g/1 lb 2 oz. fresh lamb's liver
2 tablespoons Samna (see page 19)
    or 2 tablespoons olive oil with
    a knob/pat of butter
2 garlic cloves, finely chopped
1–2 teaspoons cumin seeds
1–2 teaspoons finely chopped dried
    red chilli/chile, or 1 fresh red
    chilli/chile, deseeded and finely
    chopped
2–3 tablespoons plain/all-purpose
    flour
sea salt
1–2 lemons, cut into quarters

Serves 4

Place the pieces of liver on a chopping board and, using a sharp knife, remove the skin and any ducts. Cut the liver into thin strips.

Heat the Samna (or olive oil and butter) in a heavy-based pan. Add the garlic, cumin seeds, and dried or fresh chilli/chile and cook for 1–2 minutes.

Toss the liver in the flour, making sure the pieces are well coated and not sticking together in a clump, and add them to the pan. Fry the liver quickly, tossing it around the pan for 1–2 minutes, until lightly browned. The liver should be only just cooked, almost pinkish, so that it is tender, otherwise you end up with the texture of leather boots.

Season well with salt and tip the liver on to a serving plate. Serve immediately with lemon wedges to squeeze over it.

FOLLOWING PAGES, FROM LEFT TO RIGHT:
Pan-fried lamb's liver with cumin and lemon;
Ladies' thighs with sautéed pomegranate seeds

FISH & SHELLFISH

Prawns baked with tomatoes, peppers and cheese

Traditionally cooked in little earthenware pots, this is a popular mezze dish in the coastal regions of the Aegean and the eastern Mediterranean.

2–3 tablespoons olive oil

1 onion, cut in half lengthways and finely sliced

1 green (bell) pepper, deseeded and finely sliced

2–3 garlic cloves, finely chopped

1 fresh red chilli/chile, deseeded and finely chopped

1–2 teaspoons coriander seeds

1–2 teaspoons granulated sugar

2 x 400-g/14-oz. cans chopped tomatoes, drained

2 teaspoons white wine vinegar

a small bunch of fresh flat-leaf parsley, chopped

sea salt and freshly ground black pepper

500 g/1 lb. 2 oz. fresh, shelled prawns/shrimp, thoroughly cleaned and drained

120 g/1½ cups grated/ shredded firm, tangy cheese, such as Parmesan, Pecorino or mature Cheddar

Serves 4

Preheat the oven to 180°C (360°F) Gas 4.

Heat the oil in a heavy-based pan. Stir in the onion, (bell) pepper, garlic, chilli/chile and coriander seeds for 2–3 minutes. Add the sugar with the tomatoes and the vinegar, reduce the heat, and cook gently for 15–20 minutes, until the mixture resembles a thick sauce.

Stir in the parsley and season well with salt and pepper. Toss the prawns/shrimp in the tomato sauce to coat them, then spoon the mixture into individual pots or into an ovenproof dish. Sprinkle the cheese over each one and put them in the preheated oven for 15 minutes, until lightly browned on top.

Deep-fried whitebait with lemon

In the coastal regions of Greece, Turkey and the eastern Mediterranean countries, these tiny deep-fried fish are a great favourite, eaten whole with a squeeze of lemon.

500 g/1 lb. 2 oz. fresh whitebait

sunflower oil, for frying

4 tablespoons plain/all-purpose flour

1 scant teaspoon paprika

sea salt

a bunch of fresh flat-leaf parsley, finely chopped

1–2 lemons, cut into wedges

Serves 4

Wash and drain the fish well – if they are fresh and tiny there should be no need for any other preparation. However, if you have substituted with a slightly larger fish, you will need to scale and gut them.

Heat enough sunflower oil for deep frying in a heavy-based pan. Combine the flour, paprika and salt and toss the whitebait in the mixture, coating them in the flour, but shake off any excess. Fry the fish in batches for 2–3 minutes, until crispy and golden. Drain on paper towels.

Transfer the whitebait to a serving dish, sprinkle with salt and gently toss in the parsley. Serve with the lemon or with Zhug (see page 16) or Harissa (see page 12).

Turmeric fish balls with sunflower seeds and rocket leaves

Fish balls, or cakes, are very versatile and ideal for the mezze table. The flesh of almost any fresh fish can be used, and cans of cooked tuna work well too. Typical flavours for Middle Eastern fish balls include chillies/chiles, cumin, coriander, turmeric, saffron and cinnamon, as well as lots of fresh herbs, depending on the region they originate from. Refresh these balls with lime or lemon, or serve them with a garlicky nut sauce, or a smidgeon of Harissa (see page 12).

2 tablespoons sunflower seeds (reserve a few for garnishing)

450 g/1 lb. fresh white fish fillets, such as haddock or sea bass

2 slices day-old bread, soaked in a little water and squeezed dry

1 red onion, finely chopped

2 garlic cloves, crushed

1 fresh green or red chilli/chile, stalk and seeds removed, and finely chopped

1 teaspoon ground cumin

1–2 teaspoons ground turmeric

a small bunch of fresh flat-leaf parsley, finely chopped

a small bunch of fresh coriander/ cilantro, finely chopped (reserve a little for garnishing)

1 egg, lightly beaten

sea salt and freshly ground black pepper

3–4 tablespoons plain/all-purpose flour

2 tablespoons Samna (see page 19) or 2 tablespoons olive oil with a knob/pat of butter

a bunch of rocket/arugula leaves, rinsed and drained

1–2 limes or lemons, cut into wedges

Serves 4-6

First, dry roast the sunflower seeds. Heat a small heavy-based frying pan/skillet and toss in the sunflower seeds for 1–2 minutes, until they brown a little and emit a nutty aroma. Tip them onto a plate and put aside.

In a bowl, break up the fish fillets with a fork. Add the bread, onion, garlic, chilli/chile, cumin, turmeric and most of the sunflower seeds. Toss in the fresh herbs and mix well with the beaten the egg.

Using your hands, mould portions of the mixture into small apricot-sized balls. Toss them in the flour.

Heat the samna (or olive oil and butter) in a wide shallow frying pan/skillet and fry the fish cakes in batches until golden brown on both sides. Drain them on paper towels.

Arrange the rocket/arugula leaves and fish cakes on a dish, or wrap a leaf around each fish cake. Garnish with the reserved sprinkling of sunflower seeds and the reserved coriander/cilantro and serve with wedges of lime or lemon to squeeze over them.

Baby saffron squid stuffed with bulgur and zahtar

Popular in the coastal regions of Greece, Turkey and Lebanon, these tender baby squid, stuffed with fine-grained bulgur and flavoured with saffron and zahtar, are a delightful addition to any mezze table. Other versions include stuffing the squid with cheese and herbs and chargrilling them. To prepare the squid, hold the body sac in one hand and pull the head off with the other. Most of innards should come out with the head, but reach inside the sac with your fingers to remove any that remain in there. Whip out the transparent backbone, rinse the body sac inside and out, and pat it dry. Cut the tentacles just above the eyes, so that you have the top of the head and the tentacle joined together. Discard everything else.

50 g/¼ cup plus 1 tablespoon fine bulgur, rinsed and drained
3 tablespoons olive oil
freshly squeezed juice of 1 lemon
125 ml/½ cup white wine
a large pinch of saffron fronds
1 tablespoon tomato purée/paste
2 garlic cloves, crushed
2 teaspoons runny honey
1 tablespoon Zahtar (see page 12), reserve a little for garnishing
8 baby squid, prepared as described (see above)
sea salt and freshly ground black pepper
3–4 sprigs fresh thyme

Serves 4

Preheat the oven to 180°C (360°F) Gas 4.

Put the bulgur in a bowl and pour over just enough boiling water to cover it and no more. Place a clean tea/dish towel over the bowl and leave the bulgur for about 20 minutes to absorb the liquid. Once the water has been absorbed, the quantity of bulgur will double.

In a small bowl mix together 2 tablespoons of the olive oil with the lemon juice, white wine and saffron. Put it aside to allow the saffron to release its colour.

Combine the remaining tablespoon of olive oil with the tomato purée/paste, garlic, honey and Zahtar, and, using your fingers, rub the mixture into the bulgur and season well with salt and pepper.

Using your fingers, or a teaspoon, stuff the bulgur into the body sacs and plug the hole with the tentacles. Place the stuffed squid into a shallow earthenware or other ovenproof baking dish and pour over the saffron liquid. Tuck the sprigs of thyme around the squid and pop them in the preheated oven and bake for about 25 minutes.

Transfer the stuffed squid to a serving dish, spoon the cooking juices over them, sprinkle the reserved Zahtar over the top, and serve immediately.

Deep-fried mussels in beer batter with garlicky walnut sauce

Great street food in the ports of Istanbul, Izmir and Beirut, and classic mezze in the coastal regions, freshly caught mussels are shelled, dipped in batter, and fried in a huge, curved pan, similar to a large wok. The golden, crispy-coated, juicy mussels are often pushed onto sticks and served with a garlicky bread, or nut, sauce – you can use pistachios, almonds or pine nuts. The same idea can be applied to fresh, shelled prawns/shrimp or strips of squid.

20 fresh, shelled mussels,
   thoroughly cleaned
100 g/¾ cup plain/all-purpose flour
1 teaspoon salt
½ teaspoon bicarbonate of/baking
   soda
2 egg yolks
150 ml/⅔ cup light beer
sunflower oil, for deep frying

For the sauce:
100 g/¾ cup walnuts
2 small slices day-old white bread,
   with crusts removed, soaked in
   a little water and squeezed dry
2 garlic cloves, crushed
3 tablespoons olive oil
freshly squeezed juice of 1 lemon
1 teaspoon runny honey
a dash of white wine vinegar
salt and freshly ground black pepper

Serves 4

To make the batter, sift the flour, salt and bicarbonate of/baking soda into a bowl. Make a well in the middle and drop in the egg yolks. Gradually pour in the beer, using a wooden spoon to draw in the flour from the sides. Beat well until thick and smooth. Put aside for 30 minutes.

Meanwhile, make the sauce. Using a pestle and mortar, pound the walnuts to a paste, or whizz them in an electric blender. Add the bread and garlic and pound to a paste. Drizzle in the olive oil, stirring all the time, and beat in the lemon juice and honey. Add the dash of vinegar and season well with salt and pepper (the sauce should be creamy, so add more olive oil or a little water if it is too thick). Spoon the sauce into a serving bowl.

Heat enough oil for deep frying in a shallow pan or a wok. Using your fingers, dip each mussel into the batter and drop them into the oil. Fry them in batches until golden brown and drain on paper towels.

Thread the mussels onto small wooden skewers and serve immediately with the sauce for dipping.

SWEET MEZZE

In homes throughout Turkey and the Middle East, I have enjoyed mezze at its simplest and at its most elaborate – from a bowl of olives and a tomato purée/paste dip to whole aubergines/eggplants stuffed with quail and rice flecked with dyed-gold chickpeas – but there has always been a little bowl of something sweet, too. This might consist of a few sweet cherries picked from the tree, or ripe, fresh figs cut open and drizzled with honey, but it also might be a conserve of quince or scented rose petals, a syrupy pastry or dates stuffed with pistachio paste.

There is no real culture of dessert at the end of the meal in Turkey and the Middle East, because sweet things are often enjoyed mid-morning with a strong shot of thick black coffee or mid-afternoon with a glass of tea. Sometimes sweet mezze dishes are placed alongside little savoury mezze dishes, as many of the garlicky and spicy flavours are soothed or enhanced by a morsel of sweetness. Sweet mezze also appear late at night and they are always offered as a mark of hospitality.

Pears in saffron and cinnamon syrup

I regularly make batches of these pears and keep them in my refrigerator to pull out for my cookery workshops, or as impromptu mezze. I cut them into strips and tuck them around the Roasted Baby Peppers stuffed with Feta (see page 92) and I also use fine strips on top of yogurt dips, creamy puddings or strained yogurt. They taste great with tangy, salty and blue cheeses and cut into quarters, revealing that the flesh is golden-yellow all the way through, they grace any plate. Served whole they look decorative and appealing and rather special.

1 kg/2 lbs. 3 oz. granulated sugar
600 ml/2½ cups water
a large pinch of saffron
*   fronds/threads*
12 firm pears
5–6 small cinnamon sticks

Serves at least 8

Tip the sugar into a heavy-based saucepan and add the water and the saffron fronds. Leave the fronds to weep their dye while you prepare the pears.

Fill a bowl with cold water and keep it beside you while you peel the pears, keeping them whole with the stalks intact, and pop them into the water to prevent them from discolouring.

Heat the sugar, water and saffron and bring it to the boil, stirring all the time until the sugar dissolves. Reduce the heat, drop in the cinnamon sticks, and simmer for 10 minutes to form a syrup.

Drain the pears, shake off any excess water, and add them to the syrup. Bring the syrup to the boil, then reduce the heat and simmer the pears, rolling them from time to time in the syrup, for about 1½ hours so that the saffron colour penetrates the fruit. Leave the pears to cool in the syrup.

Pop the pears into sterilized jars, top them up with the syrup, and keep them in the refrigerator, or a cool place. They'll keep for at least 6 months. Serve them whole, quartered lengthways, or finely sliced with almost any selection of mezze dishes.

Aromatic baby aubergines in syrup

This dish must be made with baby aubergines/eggplants, which are available in some supermarkets and in Middle Eastern and African stores. Kept whole with the stalk intact, the aubergines/eggplants can be enjoyed with salty white cheese, yogurt dips and savoury pastries, devoured in one mouthful!

*8–12 firm baby aubergines/
    eggplants, with stalk intact*
*225 ml/1 cup minus 1 tablespoon
    water*
*450 g/2¼ cups granulated sugar
    (reserve 1 teaspoon)*
freshly squeezed juice of 1 lemon
25 g/1 oz. fresh ginger, finely sliced
2 cinnamon sticks
6 cardamom pods
2 pieces of mace
1–2 mastic crystals

Serves 4

Prick the aubergines/eggplants with a fork and place them in a steamer. Steam for 15 minutes, drain of any water and leave them to cool.

Meanwhile, make the syrup. Pour the water into a heavy-based pan and add the sugar and lemon juice. Bring the water to the boil, stirring all time, until the sugar has dissolved. Add the spices, reduce the heat and simmer gently for 10 minutes, until the syrup is thick and coats the back of the spoon. Crush the mastic with the reserved teaspoon of sugar and stir it into the syrup.

Gently squeeze the aubergines/eggplants to remove any excess water and place them in the syrup. Cook the aubergines/eggplants in the syrup, partially covered, on a very low heat for about 1 hour, making sure they are submerged in the syrup and that the sugar doesn't begin to burn the bottom of the pan.

Remove the pan from the heat and leave the aubergines/eggplants to cool in the syrup. To serve them, take them out and arrange them on a serving dish with the stalks pointing upwards; strain the syrup and drizzle it over them. Alternatively, you can store the aubergines/ eggplants in the strained syrup in a sealed, sterilized jar for several months.

Stuffed dates in clementine syrup

Regarded as a gift from God, dates are one of the most ancient staple foods of the Middle East and North Africa, integral to the lives of both the nomadic and settled Arabs. These stuffed dates are offered in a bowl to accompany a drink in the same way that a bowl of olives would be served.

12 moist, dried dates
12 blanched almonds
250 g/1¼ cups granulated sugar
*freshly squeezed juice of 2 clementines
    and the pared rind cut into
    thick strips*
3–4 cloves

Serves 4-6

Carefully slit each date open with a sharp knife, push the stones out and replace them with an almond.

Put the sugar into a heavy-based saucepan with the clementine juice and rind, the cloves, and 50 ml/3 tablespoons water. Gently dissolve the sugar in the liquid and bring it to the boil, reduce the heat and simmer for 5 minutes until the syrup begins to thicken. Place the stuffed dates in the syrup and poach gently for 20 minutes. Leave them to cool in the syrup.

Transfer the dates to a serving dish with the candied rind and drizzle some of the syrup over them. Serve at room temperature or chilled as part of a mezze spread.

Apricots in orange-blossom syrup with buffalo cream

Deliciously sweet and refreshing, these little bursts of divine poetry are both sophisticated and simple. Traditionally, the apricots are filled with the clotted cream of water buffalo, but they are equally good with labna or strained crème fraîche.

250 g/1½ cups plus 2 tablespoons ready-to-eat dried apricots, soaked in water for at least 6 hours, or overnight

250 g/1¼ cups granulated sugar

the pared rind of 1 lemon

2 tablespoons orange-blossom water

200 g/1 scant cup clotted buffalo cream, Labna (see page 20) or crème fraîche

1 tablespoon finely ground pistachios

Serves 4

Drain the soaked apricots and pour 250 ml/1 cup of the soaking water into a heavy-based saucepan. Tip in the sugar and bring the water to the boil, stirring all the time, until the sugar has dissolved. Boil vigorously for 1–2 minutes, then reduce the heat and stir in the lemon rind and orange-blossom water. Simmer the liquid for 5 minutes, until it begins to thicken, then slip in the apricots and poach gently for 25–30 minutes. Leave the apricots to cool in the syrup.

Lift the apricots out of the syrup with a slotted spoon and stuff each one with a teaspoonful of buffalo cream, Labna or crème fraîche. Arrange the filled apricots, cream side up, in a shallow serving dish. Cover with clingfilm/plastic wrap and pop them into the refrigerator to chill. Pour the syrup into a bowl and cover and chill it too – if you spoon the syrup over the apricots at this stage, the cream will weep into it.

Just before serving, drizzle the syrup over the filled apricots and garnish each one with a pinch of the ground pistachios.

Pumpkin poached in clove syrup with tahini

One of the best ways to enjoy pumpkin, this dish is a winter classic and utterly delicious. Traditionally served as a sweet snack with clotted buffalo cream or labna, the bitter tahini cuts the sweetness and can be mopped up along with the syrup with a chunk of bread.

450 g/2¼ cups granulated sugar

225 ml/1 cup minus 1 tablespoon water

freshly squeezed juice of 1 lemon

6–8 cloves

1 kg/2 lbs. 3 oz. peeled and deseeded pumpkin flesh, cut into cubes or rectangular blocks

1–2 tablespoons tahini

Serves 4-6

Put the sugar and water into a deep, wide heavy-based pan. Bring the liquid to the boil, stirring all the time, until the sugar has dissolved. Boil gently for 2–3 minutes, then reduce the heat and stir in the lemon juice and cloves. Simmer the liquid for 5 minutes, until it begins to thicken. Slip in the pumpkin and bring the liquid back to the boil. Reduce the heat and poach the pumpkin gently, turning the pieces over occasionally until they're tender, a rich orange colour, and gleaming – depending on the size of your pieces, this may take 1½ hours.

Leave the pumpkin to cool in the pan, then lift the pieces out of the syrup and place them on a serving dish. Drizzle some of the syrup over them and serve at room temperature, or cover and chill. Just before serving, drizzle the tahini over the pumpkin and enjoy as a sweet snack or as part of a mezze spread.

PREVIOUS PAGES, FROM LEFT TO RIGHT: Apricots in orange-blossom syrup with buffalo cream; Pumpkin poached in clove syrup with tahini; Aromatic baby aubergines in syrup; Stuffed dates in clementine syrup

Grated quince conserve with labna, allspice and nutmeg

In countries like Greece, Turkey, Iran and Lebanon where there are fertile valleys offering abundant fruit harvests, the list of conserves is endless. Perhaps the king of all conserves is the one made with the bright yellow, scented quinces, as the result is rich, vibrant and perfumed. To grate the quince, you need a traditional bronze grater or a plastic one, because the regular metal kitchen grater reacts with the fruit and tarnishes the flavour. Alternatively, you can use the grating implement on a food processor or a sharp knife to cut the flesh into thin strips. The grated quince conserve is often served in little saucers on its own, with a decorative spoon to eat it with, or with chunks of crusty bread, and as a sweet mezze dish it can be spooned over labna (yogurt cheese) and dusted with spices.

freshly squeezed juice of 2 lemons
1 kg/2 lbs. fresh quince, peeled, cored
   and coarsely grated
900 g/4½ cups granulated sugar
2 tablespoons runny honey
Labna (see page 20), to serve
allspice and fresh nutmeg, to serve

Serves at least 8

Fill a bowl with cold water and squeeze in the juice of half a lemon. Peel, core and coarsely grate the quinces. Stir the grated flesh in the lemon water as you grate each quince to prevent it from discolouring.

Pour 500 ml/2 cups water into a heavy-based pot and stir in the sugar. Bring the water to the boil, stirring all the time, until the sugar dissolves. Add the rest of the lemon juice, reduce the heat, and simmer for 10 minutes to form a syrup.

Drain the grated quince and stir it into the syrup. Bring it to the boil, reduce the heat, and simmer for 25–30 minutes. Stir in the honey and continue to simmer for 15 minutes. Leave the conserve to cool in the pot. Spoon it into sterilized jars and store them in a cool place for at least 6 months.

To serve as mezze, put a dollop of chilled, creamy Labna into individual shallow bowls, dust the top with a little allspice, and spoon some of the quince preserve on top. Grate a little nutmeg over the quince and enjoy the layered flavours.

Plum tomato and almond conserve

Prepared with small, firm plum tomatoes, this sweet conserve is a perfect accompaniment to mezze dishes. Most people are familiar with savoury tomato chutneys, but not necessarily with a syrupy tomato conserve that goes well with chunks of warm, crusty bread, labna, salty cheeses and thick dips like hummus. To blanch the almonds, put them into a bowl and pour over enough boiling water to cover them. Leave them to steep and soften for at least 6 hours – I often leave them for 24 hours – changing the water from time to time. Using your fingertips, rub off the skins to reveal the blanched almond.

500 g/5¼ oz. small, firm plum tomatoes
450 g/2¼ cups granulated sugar
150 ml/⅔ cup water
2 tablespoons whole blanched almonds
6–8 whole cloves
crusty bread, to serve

Serves 6-8

First, prepare the tomatoes by carefully submerging them for a few seconds in boiling water, then plunge them straight away into a bowl of cold water to halt the cooking. Peel off the skins.

Place the skinned tomatoes in a heavy-based pan and cover with the sugar. Leave them to sit for 2 hours to draw out some of the juices. If there is not much juice, you might have to add a little more water.

Add the water to the pan and place it over the heat, stirring gently until the sugar dissolves. Bring the syrup to the boil for a few minutes, skim off any froth, and reduce the heat. Stir in the almonds and cloves and simmer gently for about 30 minutes, stirring from time to time.

Turn off the heat and leave the syrup to cool in the pan. Spoon the conserve into sterilized jars and store in a cool place. To serve, spoon it into a bowl and enjoy it with chunks of crusty bread.

Dried fig, rakı and pine nut conserve

This is a wonderful winter conserve and a great way to use dried figs. I used to eat it with hot fresh bread, straight from the baker's oven, in the cold morning air in Bursa before heading up the mountain to ski. The addition of the aniseed-flavoured spirit, 'rakı', ('arak' in Arabic, 'ouzo' in Greek) is optional – you can omit it altogether and increase the amount of water or you can substitute it with brandy or whisky. Spoon the jam over warm bread and Labna (see page 20), or serve it with salty cheese and cured meats.

450 g/2¼ cups granulated sugar
225 ml/1 cup minus 1 tablespoon
   water
500 g/1 lb. 2 oz. dried figs,
   coarsely chopped
3 tablespoons pine nuts
100 ml/½ cup minus 1 tablespoon
   rakı

Serves 6–8

Put the sugar and water into a heavy-based pan. Bring the liquid to the boil, stirring all the time, until the sugar has dissolved. Reduce the heat and simmer for 5–10 minutes, until the syrup begins to thicken.

Stir in the figs. Bring the liquid to the boil once more, then reduce the heat and simmer for 20 minutes, until the figs are tender. Add the pine nuts and rakı and simmer for a further 10 minutes.

Leave the conserve to cool in the pan. Spoon it into sterilized jars and store in a cool, dry place for at least 6 months. To serve, spoon it into a bowl and enjoy it with crusty bread, cheese and cured meats.

Creamed tahini with grape syrup

Tahini, the thick paste made with crushed sesame seeds, is used in a variety ways in Greece, Turkey and the Middle East – not just in the ubiquitous chickpea purée, hummus! It is drizzled over sweet and savoury dishes; combined with lemon and garlic in dips and dressings; it is sweetened with honey or a fruit molasses to fill pastries and doughs; and it is pounded with sugar and nuts to make halva and other sweetmeats. On a daily basis, it is beaten with a fruit molasses made from grapes, dates, mulberries, or carob and eaten with bread for breakfast, or as a snack, or as part of a mezze spread. Called 'tahin pekmez' in Turkish, it is the region's answer to peanut butter!

4–5 tablespoons light or dark tahini
2–3 tablespoons grape or date molasses (or runny honey)
feta cubes, olives and chunks of crusty bread, to serve

Serves 4

In a bowl, beat the tahini until it is smooth. Swirl in the molasses to your taste – the perfect combination for me is 2 tablespoons tahini to 1 tablespoon grape molasses, but some people prefer it sweeter or less sweet.

Drizzle a little of the molasses over the top and serve it with feta cubes, olives and chunks of crusty bread.

NOTE: You can turn 'tahin pekmez' into a savoury dip by adding the juice of 1 lemon, 1 teaspoon dried mint and, if you like, a crushed garlic clove – the mixture might require a splash of water to thin it down as the lemon juice stiffens it up. I was once enjoying a bowl of sweet tahin pekmez with some friends when the cook came over to the table and altered it to a savoury dip, just like that, to accompany the next dishes.

Date, pistachio and coconut truffles with honey

Throughout the Arab world, dates are offered as a mark of hospitality in the form of a sweetmeat, such as these delicious truffles, which keep well in the refrigerator. The best varieties of date for sweet and savoury mezze are the soft, ready-to-eat ones or the large, fleshy Medjool.

250 g/2 cups minus 1 tablespoon
   shelled, unsalted pistachios
250 g/2 scant cups stoned/pitted
   dates, roughly chopped
2 teaspoons ground cinnamon
2 teaspoons rosewater
1 tablespoon runny honey
3 tablespoons desiccated coconut

Serves 6–8

Dry roast the pistachios in a small, heavy-based frying pan/skillet, until they emit a nutty aroma. Using a pestle and mortar, or an electric blender, coarsely grind the pistachios.

Add the dates with the cinnamon and pound, or blend, them with the ground pistachios to form a thick paste. Drizzle in the rosewater and honey while you are doing this to help loosen the mixture, although it will become stickier.

Once the paste is fairly smooth, dampen your fingers and take small portions into your hands and mould them into cherry-sized balls. Spread the desiccated coconut on a plate and roll the little truffles in it, making sure they are evenly coated.

Pop the truffles into a sealed container and keep in the refrigerator until you are ready to use them. They can be served chilled or at room temperature and go well with salty and spicy mezze dishes. The truffles will keep for 2–3 weeks in the fridge.

Semolina helwah with pine nuts and cinnamon

'Helwah' ('helva' in Turkish) simply means 'sweet' in Arabic and there are many variations of this sweet dish usually consisting of flour, semolina, or tahini ('tahina') combined with nuts and sugar. It is regarded as a bearer of good luck and is associated with celebrations and religious festivals.

225 g/2 sticks salted butter
450 g/3½ cups coarsely ground
   semolina
3 tablespoons pine nuts
850 ml/3¼ cups plus 3 tablespoons
   milk
225 g/1 cup plus 2 tablespoons
   granulated sugar
1–2 teaspoons ground cinnamon

Serves 6–8

Melt the butter in a heavy-based pan. Stir in the semolina and pine nuts. Cook until lightly browned, stirring all the time.

Reduce the heat and pour in the milk. Mix well, cover the pan with a clean tea/dish towel and press the lid down tightly. Pull up the flaps of the tea/dish towel over the lid and simmer gently, until the milk has been absorbed.

Add the sugar, stirring until it has dissolved. Cover the pan again with the tea/dish towel and lid and remove from the heat. Leave to stand for 30 minutes, tossing it occasionally with a wooden spoon.

Spoon the halva into little bowls – you don't have to serve it all at once, as it keeps well and can be nibbled as a snack over a few days. Dust each one with cinnamon and serve the halva at the end of a mezze spread or in combination with feta, savoury pastries, stuffed vine leaves, and a purée or salad.

Golden couscous with saffron, pistachios and honey

Couscous is the national dish of Morocco, and in the Maghreb region, which includes Tunisia and Algeria, it is regarded as an institution. Sweet couscous is enjoyed as a snack, or as a course on its own during a meal, but it can also be added to the mezze mix. Piled in a mound on a plate, it is by its very nature a dish to share, using your fingers to deftly roll and flick the grains into your mouth, or by tucking into the communal dish with small spoons.

400 ml/1½ cups plus 2 tablespoons hot water

1 teaspoon salt

a large pinch of saffron fronds/threads

350 g/2 cups fine couscous

2–3 tablespoons sultanas/golden raisins

2–3 tablespoons rosewater

1 tablespoon sunflower oil

1 teaspoon ground cinnamon

½ teaspoon ground cloves

50 g/3 tablespoons slightly salted butter

2–3 tablespoons shelled, unsalted pistachios

1–2 tablespoons runny honey

Serves 6–8

Stir the salt and saffron fronds into the water and leave it to colour and cool a little, until lukewarm. Tip the couscous into a bowl and pour the water over the couscous, making sure all the grains are submerged in it. Cover the bowl with a dampened tea/dish towel and leave the couscous to absorb the water for 15 minutes.

In a small bowl, soak the sultanas/golden raisins in the rosewater and put aside.

Rake the couscous grains with a fork to separate them, then gently rub in the oil with your fingertips, lifting the grains into the air and letting them fall back down to aerate them. Rub in the cinnamon and the ground cloves.

Drain the sultanas/golden raisins and add them to the couscous. Toss well and tip the couscous onto a serving dish – you can pile it high with your fingers, or shape it into a mound by pressing the couscous into a bowl or the conical lid of a tagine, placing the serving dish upside down on top, inverting it, and lifting the bowl or lid off.

Melt the butter in a heavy-based frying pan/skillet and stir in the pistachios, until they emit a nutty aroma. Spoon the nuts over and around the couscous and drizzle the butter over the top.

Starting at the top of the dome, drizzle the honey in lines down the sides, and serve with individual spoons to make it easy to tuck into.

FOLLOWING PAGES, FROM LEFT TO RIGHT: Date, pistachio and coconut truffles with honey; Golden couscous with saffron, pistachios and honey; Semolina helwah with pine nuts and cinnamon.

Syrupy cheese sponges with candied orange and lemon

These delectable cheese sponges can be served on their own as a sweet snack, as the finale to mezze or as a prominent part of the spread. Syrupy, with a hint of salt from the feta, the sponges are very moist and moreish and add an intriguing and satisfying touch to a selection of lighter mezze dishes.

125 g/1 cup plain/all-purpose or
    semolina flour
1 tablespoon icing/confectioners'
    sugar
1 scant teaspoon bicarbonate
    of/baking soda
50 g/3 tablespoons butter
200 g/7 oz. feta, crumbled
1 egg

For the syrup:
225 g/1 cup plus 1 tablespoon
    granulated sugar
240 ml/1 cup water
*freshly squeezed juice of 1 lemon
    and rind, finely shredded into
    thin threads*
*rind of 1 orange, finely shredded into
    thin threads*

Serves 6

Preheat the oven to 180°C (360°F) Gas 4 and lightly grease a baking pan.

Heat the sugar and water in heavy based pot, stirring all the time until the sugar has dissolved. Bring the water to the boil, stir in the lemon juice and both of the shredded rinds. Reduce the heat and simmer for 15–20 minutes.

Meanwhile, sift the flour, icing/confectioners' sugar, and bicarbonate of/baking soda into a bowl and rub in the butter until it resembles fine breadcrumbs. Make a hollow in the middle and drop in the feta and the egg. Draw the flour over the top and, using your hands, knead the mixture into a sticky dough.

Rinse your hands but keep them dampened. Mould the dough into small balls, place them at intervals in the greased baking pan – they need a little room to expand – and pop them in the preheated oven for about 25 minutes.

Pour the hot syrup over the sponges, making sure they are all covered with the candied rind, and return them to the oven for 5–10 minutes. Leave the sponges to cool in the baking pan and soak up the syrup.

Serve the sponges chilled or at room temperature. If you like, add them to a mezze spread with dips, salads, pastries, olives and a bowl of fresh fruit.

Shredded pastry filled with cheese in lemon syrup

Of all of the traditional sweet, syrupy pastries, this one is my favourite, with its melted cheese and hint of lemon. Called 'konafa' ('kunefe' or 'kadayif' in Turkish), it is made with thin strands of pastry, similar in appearance to vermicelli. Unfortunately, they are almost impossible to make at home, as the batter requires tossing through a sieve/strainer onto a hot metal sheet over an open fire, but you can buy packets of ready-prepared strands in Middle Eastern, Turkish and Greek food stores; you can also buy individual non-stick pans that are specifically designed for making konafa. The pastry is called 'kadaif', which is also the name given to many of the sweet dishes prepared with it. The cheese most commonly used for konafa – dil peyniri – has a slightly rubbery texture and can be pulled apart into strings, so the standard pizza mozzarella is an ideal substitute. Perfect for the mezze table or, in fact, at any time of day, konafa is a sweet dish for reunions and celebrations – in other words, a dish to be shared.

225 g/8 oz. ready-prepared kadaif

120 g/4 oz. Samna (see page 19), melted

350 g/12½ oz. dil peyniri, or mozzarella, thinly sliced

1–2 tablespoons shelled pistachios, coarsely ground

For the syrup:

225 g/1 cup plus 1 tablespoon granulated sugar

125 ml/½ cup water

freshly squeezed juice of 1 lemon

Serves 4–6

Preheat the oven to 180°C (360°F) Gas 4.

First prepare the syrup. Put the sugar and water into a pan and bring it to the boil, stirring until the sugar has dissolved. Add the lemon juice, reduce the heat, and leave the syrup to simmer and thicken for about 15 minutes, until it coats the back of the wooden spoon. Turn off the heat and leave the syrup to cool. Chill it in the refrigerator if you like.

Put the kadaif into a bowl and separate the strands. Pour the melted Samna over them and, using your fingers, rub it all over the strands so they are coated in it. Spread half the pastry in the base of a shallow baking pan (the Turks use a round pan roughly 27 cm/11 in. in diameter) and press it down with your fingers. Lay the slices of cheese over the top and cover with the rest of the pastry, pressing it down firmly and tucking it down the sides.

Place the pan in the preheated oven and bake the pastry for about 45 minutes, until it is golden brown. Loosen the edges of the pastry with a sharp knife and pour the cold syrup over it – the hot pastry will absorb most of the syrup but you can pop it back into the oven for 2–3 minutes to ensure that it does. Scatter the pistachios over the top. Divide the pastry into squares or segments, depending on the shape of your baking pan, and serve while still hot, so that the cheese remains melted and soft.

Ladies' navels

This is one of a series of classic deep-fried pastries bathed in syrup. A creation of the Ottoman Palace kitchens, the dough is shaped like a ring, similar to a small, modern doughnut/donut, hence the pastry's name. The same dough can be shaped into other treats with wonderfully evocative names, like Vezir's Fingers, Beauty's Lips, and Tulumba, which are little twists piped through a fluted nozzle. Ladies' Navels are often served with clotted buffalo cream and chopped pistachios but, because they are so sweet, I think the tartness of Labna or crème fraîche or the saltiness of crumbled feta complement them better. Serve these at the end of a mezze spread, or alongside light savoury dishes.

250 ml/1 cup water
50 g/3 tablespoons butter
½ teaspoon salt
175 g/1 cup plus 3 tablespoons
   plain/all-purpose flour
50 g/3 tablespoons semolina
2 eggs
sunflower oil

For the syrup:
450 g/2¼ cups granulated sugar
225 ml/1 cup minus 1 tablespoon
   water
freshly squeezed juice of 1 lemon

Serves 4–6

First prepare the syrup. Put the sugar and water in a heavy-based pan and bring to the boil, stirring all the time. Stir in the lemon juice and reduce the heat. Simmer for 10–15 minutes, until it has thickened a little, then leave it to cool.

Put the water, butter and salt into a heavy-based pan and bring it to the boil. Remove from the heat and add the flour and semolina, beating all the time, until the mixture becomes smooth and leaves the side of the pan. Leave the mixture to cool, then beat in the eggs so that it gleams. Add 1 tablespoon of the cooled syrup and beat well.

Heat up enough oil for deep frying in a heavy-based frying pan/skillet, or a curved pan like a wok, until it is just warm. Remove the pan from the heat. Wet your fingers, as the dough is sticky, and pick up an apricot-sized piece of dough, roll it into a ball, flatten it in the palm of your hand, and use your finger to make an indentation in the middle to resemble a lady's navel. Drop the dough into the pan of warmed oil. Repeat with the rest of the mixture.

Place the pan over the heat. As the oil heats up, the pastries will swell with the dip in the middle. Swirl the oil, so that the Ladies' Navels turn golden all over. Drain the navels through a wire sieve/strainer, or on paper towels, before tossing them into the cooled syrup. Leave them in the syrup for a few minutes.

Arrange the Ladies' Navels on a serving dish, spoon some of the syrup over and around them, and serve with a dollop of labna, crème fraîche or crumbled feta.

Mini mastic-flavoured rice puddings

Creamy rice pudding is one of those home-cooked comfort foods, served hot or cold, but these little pots of pudding reveal an intriguing hint of resin derived from the mastic crystals. Traditional rice puddings from the region are usually flavoured with vanilla, cinnamon or rose water, but the mastic-flavoured ones are perfect for mezze. Make them a feature of any mezze spread so that their presence is noted and can be reached for whenever you feel the urge for a spoonful of creamy indulgence to slip exquisitely down your throat.

2 mastic crystals
100 g/½ cup granulated sugar
60 g/⅓ cup short-grain rice or
   pudding rice, rinsed thoroughly
   and drained
1 litre/quart whole milk
60 g/½ cup rice flour
icing/confectioners' sugar, for dusting

Serves at least 8

Using a small pestle and mortar, pulverize the mastic crystals with 1 teaspoon of the sugar, until they are ground to a powder. Put it aside.

Tip the rice into a deep, heavy-based saucepan. Pour in enough water to just cover the rice and bring it to the boil. Reduce the heat and simmer until the water has been absorbed.

Pour in the milk and bring it to the boil, stirring all the time. Reduce the heat and simmer until the liquid begins to thicken and the rice sticks to the back of a wooden spoon. Add the rest of the sugar and the ground mastic, stirring all the time until both of them have dissolved.

In a small bowl, slake the rice powder with a little water to make a smooth paste. Stir in a ladleful of the hot liquid, then tip it immediately into the milk, stirring all the time, to prevent any lumps from forming. Keep simmering and stirring for about 15 minutes, until the liquid is very thick and the rice is visible throughout and coats the back of the spoon.

Spoon the mixture into individual pots – if you have too much for the number of guests, you can always tip the rest into a bowl to serve as a dessert on another occasion. Leave the rice puddings to cool and allow a skin to form on top. Then cover them and put in the refrigerator to chill. When you are ready to add them to the mezze table, dust each one with a little icing/confectioners' sugar and lay out some small spoons beside them.

Burnt chicken breast puddings with cinnamon

It might sound strange and possibly unappealing to be offering a dessert prepared with chicken breast, but I can assure you that this traditional delight from the Ottoman Palace kitchens is not only surprising, it is utterly scrumptious. Crucial to the pleasure of the dish are the fine threads of cooked chicken, which must be thin enough to add texture but not so thick that they are detectably meaty. For no reason other than novelty, these are well worth trying – and you might even be won over!

1 chicken breast
5 tablespoons rice flour
850 ml/3¼ cups plus 3 tablespoons milk
300 ml/1¼ cups single/light cream
a pinch of salt
175 g/1 cup minus 2 tablespoons granulated sugar
ground cinnamon, for dusting

Serves at least 8

Place the chicken breast in a saucepan with enough water to just cover it. Bring the water to the boil, then reduce the heat and simmer until the breast is cooked. Drain the breast and tear it into very, very fine threads.

In a bowl, slake the rice flour with a little of the milk to form a smooth paste, the consistency of thick double/heavy cream. Pour the rest of the milk and the cream into a heavy-based pan. Add the salt and sugar and bring it to the boil, stirring all the time, until the sugar has dissolved. Add a ladleful of the hot milk to the slaked rice flour, then tip it all into the pan and stir vigorously. Reduce the heat, stirring all the time, until the mixture begins to thicken. Gently beat in the threads of chicken and continue to simmer until the mixture is very thick.

Lightly grease a wide, non-stick, heavy-based frying pan/skillet and place it over the heat. When hot, tip the mixture into it and keep it over the heat for about 2 minutes to brown, or slightly burn, the bottom of the mixture – you can check by gently levering up an edge to peep beneath. Reduce the heat and move the pan around for 2–3 minutes to make sure the bottom is evenly browned – a little bit burnt is fine, but you are not looking for charred! Turn off the heat and leave the mixture to cool in the pan.

Using a sharp-pointed knife, cut the pudding into small rectangles. Lift each rectangle out of the pan using a spatula, and place them on a flat surface, burnt-side down. Roll each one over slightly, like rolling someone over in bed, so that the burnt side is up and the two long edges of the rectangle form a seam underneath. Place them seam-side down on a serving dish, cover them, and keep in the refrigerator.

When you are ready to eat them, dust the tops with cinnamon and serve them as a surprise at the end of a mezze spread, or alongside light dips, salads, feta and fruit.

AFTER MEZZE

As mezze can be enjoyed at any time of the day, it is traditionally accompanied by glasses of sweet tea or a chilled fruit sherbet. However, mezze made its mark in history by soaking up the spirits imbibed by male travellers and nobility and, for those who drink alcohol, it is a leisurely style of eating that marries so perfectly with a beer, a glass of wine or the regional aniseed-flavoured drink, 'arak' or 'rakı'. When mezze is presented as a complete meal, the enjoyment of it is completed by a herbal tea, such as mint or sage, to aid the digestion, or by a traditional strong black coffee following the method of the Turks or the Arabs.

Honey raki

The regional aniseed-flavoured spirit, 'arak' ('rakı' in Turkish), is generally drunk before and during eating. It is a clear spirit, but when water is added it turns cloudy, which is why it earned its moniker, 'lion's milk'. Depending on your company, there are certain rituals in the drinking of arak – a bit like Scotch whisky purists, there are some who like it neat, others prefer it cloudy; there are some who drink it on the rocks and there are those who insist upon two glasses – one for the spirit, the other for water. For after mezze there is a tradition of drinking the spirit as a 'digestif' by flavouring it with honey and serving it chilled. In the Greek islands, where the plain spirit is called 'ouzo', this delectable honey version is called 'raki'.

300 ml/10 fl. oz arak, ouzo, or rakı
3–4 teaspoons runny honey

Serves 4

Pour the arak into a pot and heat it up with the honey, until it dissolves. Bring it to scalding point and pour it into a small bottle or jug/pitcher and put it in the refrigerator to chill. Pour the honey raki into little shot glasses and enjoy sipping it after you have finished your mezze.

Moroccan mint tea

Mint tea, 'atay bi na'na' is Morocco's national drink, and is offered throughout the day in people's homes, in cafés and restaurants, in the markets, during a meal and at the end of one. Served sweet – you can adapt the sweetness to your taste – the tea is generally drunk from small, ornate glasses, often fitted into little holders, and the teapot is held close to the glass and gradually raised higher and higher to create a sense of ceremony as well as to produce a little froth on top of each glass. On festive occasions, two teapots, one in each hand, will be held above the glass to be raised with a skilful flourish that creates a thick froth on top. This traditional mint tea, literally packed with fresh mint leaves on their stalks (add a few springs of lemon verbena if you have any), is a delightfully refreshing and cleansing way to finish off the pleasures of the mezze table.

1–1½ tablespoons loose green tea
roughly 6 cane sugar lumps
a very large handful of fresh mint
    leaves (garden mint and
    peppermint) on their stalks

Makes a pot for 4–6

Pour some boiling water into the teapot to heat it. Swirl the water around and pour it out. Place the tea and half the sugar in the pot and pour in a little boiling water to steep the leaves for a few minutes.

Grab the bunch of mint leaves and snap the stalks so that you can ram the whole lot into the pot, literally stuffing it full of mint. Add the rest of the sugar and fill the pot to the brim with boiling water. Cover with a tea cosy or, if flame resistant, place the pot over a very low heat to allow the sugar to dissolve and the tea to infuse for 5–10 minutes.

Pour some of the tea into a glass and then pour it back into the pot. Do this several times to make sure the flavours of the mint and green tea mingle. Place 4–6 tea glasses side by side, hold the teapot just above the first glass and, as you pour, raise the teapot higher to create a little froth on the surface. Continue with the other glasses and serve while the tea is hot.

Turkish coffee

Traditionally, coffee is a prestigious drink and not everyone can afford to enjoy it often. In some communities, it is reserved for special occasions and in eastern Anatolia, there still exists the tradition of selecting a suitable bride based on her ability to prepare and serve coffee, while the prospective mother-in-law and her son inspect the young girl's beauty and grace. The traditional cooking vessel for Turkish coffee, as well as for Greek, Lebanese and Arab coffee, is a slim, deep pot (called 'cezve' in Turkish), often made out of tin-lined copper, with a long handle. Generally medium-roast Arabica coffee beans are passed through a very fine grinder until they're almost powdery. Turkish coffee is always drunk black in small cups; sometimes it's already sweetened or, alternatively, sugar lumps are served on the side to hold between the teeth and suck the coffee through it.

To make the coffee, measure the water by the coffee cup (a standard, small cylindrical cup) and the coffee by the teaspoon. The general rule allows for one coffee cup of water to one teaspoon of coffee and one teaspoon of sugar per person. Tip the water into the pot and spoon the coffee and sugar on the top (omit the sugar if you prefer your coffee unsweetened). Use a teaspoon to quickly stir the sugar and coffee into the surface of the water to give the desired froth a kick-start. Put the pan over a medium heat and, using the teaspoon, gradually scrape the outer edges of the surface into the middle to create an island of froth. The key to froth is to always work at the surface, never touch the bottom of the pot with a spoon. Once the coffee is hot, pour about a third of it into the coffee cup to warm it up and return the pan to the heat. Continue to gather the froth in the middle and, just as the coffee begins to bubble up, take it off the heat and pour it into the cup. Leave the coffee cup to stand for 1 minute to let the coffee grains settle, and then drink it while it is hot.

Lebanese coffee with cardamom

Lebanese coffee is very similar to Turkish coffee, although it is traditionally flavoured with cardamom. You can buy the finely ground, powdery coffee required to make Turkish or Lebanese coffee in most Middle Eastern stores and some delicatessens. It is also prepared in a long-handled pot, called a 'rakweh' in Arabic, and it is generally served already sweetened. Prepare the coffee in the same way as the Turkish version but add the seeds of 2 cardamom pods to the pot with the sugar. There is also a cinnamon version, made by adding a small cinnamon stick to the pot, or by adding a small amount of ground cinnamon to the ground coffee.

INDEX

ACKNOWLEDGMENTS

Mezze is undoubtedly my favourite food
and I have many joyous memories of sharing
little dishes with good friends, but I would
particularly like to mention my old friend,
Hasan Selamet, who takes me on a tour of
the traditional 'meze houses' every time I'm in
Istanbul. I would also like to thank Julia Charles,
Nathan Joyce and Toni Kay for their support in
getting this book off the ground and steering it
in the right direction, and I would like to thank
Jan Baldwin for her fresh, striking photographs
which capture the philosophy of mezze.